Handsome, Successful, 33, and Depressed

G. VANSTONE

Fulton Books, Inc.
Meadville, PA

Published by Fulton Books 2020

ISBN 978-1-64952-113-2 (paperback)
ISBN 978-1-64952-114-9 (digital)

Printed in the United States of America

PART 1

If everything's so fucking great, how come I feel so shit? Two cars, two houses, and two kids. Maybe De La Soul were right? Is three the magic number?

I'm currently going through these times, times when in which, these sad clouds seem to just hit me; they overcome me, and I sink into what feels like a total numbness. A dark miserable holiday arrives, and I'm booked in—first-class, all-inclusive—for the whole cruise trip. and there seems to be no getting off. So far I think I've managed it quite well so that the people around me don't notice. I'm good at acting like everything is fine; I hide these clouds from the world, and I hide them well. Saying that, I do cry a lot, inside and out, and here lies a problem. You see, when you cry on the inside, no one can notice and no one can help. When you cry on the outside, everyone notices, but no one wants to help. People aren't programmed to help a fully grown man who cries. Nor are they programmed to care. So when these times arrive—without much warning I hasten to add— your personality drowns and suffocates from an onrushing wall of darkness. Inside you die, and let's face it, no one feels empathy for the dead, just for the people left behind. So when the clouds come, I end up just walking around in a bubble of despair. Distractions don't help as there is nothing that can distract you from your own despair. The TV's on; I've been watching it for over an hour, but I couldn't tell you what's happening or the name of the program or anyone who's in it. Work's a day-on-day battle split between drinking, meeting friends, and crying outside on the stairwells or upstairs where we have empty floors that are above the one I work on. Our building isn't full by any means; we have about ten empty floors that someday will be filled by an international newspaper.

I'm not always under the cloud; I just have episodes which I call Wobbles. They just sort of pop up. I'm not taking drugs for it either because drugs are for the people with real problems, where there's a real issue. For now, I just carry on; I'm sure it'll go away at some point. I hope it'll go away; I pray it'll go away.

So why me? What did I do? Who am I to be the lucky winner of a "shitty feeling" lotto ticket? I have a decent job, a job so easy a monkey could do it. A job that, for no reason I can fathom, pays a ridiculously large salary. I have a beautiful wife and two nice kids— all the markings of a happy life. A quick note here: when someone says "beautiful wife and kids," their views are usually clouded. In this instance, it's the whole truth and nothing but the truth. My kids, for example, people are constantly telling me how beautiful they are. Other people actually like my kids. Seriously, no one likes other people's kids, but people like mine. They're handsome little fellas. They play nicely and have friends at nursery who also really like them. Even the teachers like them!

My wife, I adore. Plus she's gorgeous, sexy as hell. I know this as I wouldn't go out with (let alone marry) a Munter. I know this as I have an internal issue where I can't actually speak to ugly people. If the situation ever arises, I just have to walk off. Ask Mo Decon, he's seen this issue applied during social outings. We, me and Mo, once had a mutual colleague who was very funny, intelligent, and had great stories from around the world. Everyone liked her. She had a boyfriend and was an all-round popular person. But I couldn't talk to her. I happen to find something that was wrong with her face that just said to me "Minger," and I couldn't talk to her. Does this mean that I am shallow? Yep.

From the moment my wife wakes, she's beautiful. I don't know how—some genetic bodily setup thingy I guess. If my wife were to have gone out on a night that would've killed Oliver Reed (before he did it himself), she would wake the following morning looking better than Angelina Jolie attending the Oscars.

When we first met, I had to up my game—basically lie—just to get any sort of attention from her. She is very much out of my league, so I told her I was a firefighter. It seemed to do the trick. I have fessed up since. I couldn't realistically carry it off for long. I'm too unfit, plus I'm not the real-life hero type. I do, however, actually believe that I was a firefighter for about an hour or so on that fateful evening. We both just got on. We had a nice time and enjoyed our company straight off the bat, if you will. I think it was down to the fact that we had a common ground from the start: she liked me and I did too.

Since we met, we got married, had kids, and have filled our lives with meaningless crap—filled it with lots and lots of meaningless crap. We have a sports car; a family car; a motorbike "for fun"; a holiday home; and whacking great big HD, 3D, fucking double-D plasma screens all over the house. Granted, I wanted most of that; my wife prefers sofas and nice bedding. We live in a smallish village, which I like and my family likes. We have local stores in which you get overcharged and have to wait forever to get anything, but you do get a nice chat thrown in. There's no real crime; I think that the last big criminal activity issue was damage to a pot plant near the fountain. It has a spacious beach that is kept clean, and we even have an award-winning chip shop!

So I'm lucky I guess. Am I lucky…am I…? There are people a hell of a lot worse off than me. But I have different forms of luck. Most of my luck is a creation of my own doing, good and bad. On the strength of this prognosis, I'm pretty sure I'm lucky. But also, on the strength of "it's my own doing," then I'm positive I'm a bad-luck generating machine. I constantly have bad ideas but usually fail to realize the badness until it's too late. If there were such a machine as a "bad-idea generator," it would be called the Martin Alberts bad-idea generator. Or a play on those words, you know, something a bit snappier. I do have good ideas; they just turn bad. The meaning is always (or usually) to do good, but it all tends to go pear-shaped at some point. Like the time that I set fire to the pond of my friend's father. I'll explain that later. Maybe my ideas are good and my luck's just bad. I hadn't thought of it like that before. Maybe. One of the big problems is that I'm not young and stupid, I'm middle-aged and stupid. The benefits of this are as follows:

1. You always think you're right, straight off the bat.
2. You don't have to be home early so you can see the bad idea through.
3. You can financially fund most bad ideas.
4. You can afford to run away from most bad ideas.

Anyway, I digress, my life's not just about bad ideas and good or bad luck. I also see myself as a crusader, a man for the people! Someone who stands up for the little guy, mainly against London transport, but still… My wife would say I complain, I say I crusade. So here I am, a middle-aged bad-idea generator, having Wobbles and saving the world. My family does put up with a lot I guess, but I pro-vide—I work, sort of. And seeing that I do, what's wrong with chas-ing the odd bus driver across London Bridge? I'll explain that, along with the pond fire, later also. My wife would say I'm immature. "An emotional cripple," she once called me. But if you can find a woman who doesn't think men are in general a bit nobbish, I'll give you fifty quid. Fact is I'm probably just like most. I just happen to lack a few things, like tact and subtlety. Oh, and I can't keep secrets—never, never, never tell me secrets. Ranting. I'm now ranting, this is how the Wobbles start. Rants go on and on. The only way I can stop them is to sleep. Sleep stops me from thinking, stops me from crying, stops me full stop.

I ask myself, how did I get to where I am now? When did the Wobbles begin? When did I start getting hit with these clouds of doom that suck the smile from my face and the hope from my soul? Sounds dramatic, right? Well, you sit through one of them and then tell me any different. These Wobbles manage to stop me from talking aloud to others, yet they make me talk constantly to myself. Sometimes there doesn't seem to be room for the talk outside of my own head. Conversations going on and on, around and around, inside my head—it's like a chat room full to the brim with me's in it, hundreds of me's nattering on or screaming or shouting or crying. I recall this one event when the times went from good to bad. This has to be the starting point, must be…

PART 2

ABOUT TWO YEARS AGO

I should have been a pro at this by now. This was round about the tenth time I'd moved houses in the past five years or so. Sadly, I had greatly underestimated this move. I had underestimated the size of the van needed, the level of crapness the solicitors would be at, the battery power of a mobile phone, and my wife's reactions. Also, having a six-month-old who had only recently been allowed home from the hospital, a postnatal depressed wife, and a mother-in-law all in tow didn't help. I guess, looking back, the signs of this being a challenge were all there. But hey ho, I didn't see them. The sun is shining, so onwards and upwards! I thought.

Somehow, we had managed to get the keys to the new house a week or so before the move day. I say somehow—I knew how we'd got them just not how we'd managed to keep them. My wife had asked the agents if we could borrow the keys so we could have another viewing and to clean it up a bit. The place had been empty for the best part of a year. Mice and dust were running rampant, so we took the keys and never gave them back. Ever. We had spent the week nipping back and forth, cleaning and moving a few items in and out—nothing major. This was all done before completing on the property with the mortgage company.

The morning of the move was a bright one. We were getting set to leave suburbia and enter village life, and everyone seemed excited. I had already taken one van load the one-hundred-mile round trip the night before to break the back of the removal. I don't like paying for things that I think I can do myself; hence, I hired a van and got stuck in. I had initially thought the van would be sufficient for one if not two trips; I was wrong.

My brother rolled up to help out that morning, and upon his arrival, I declared, "I'm not used to all this manual labor, I'm an office bod."

"Well, stop moving house then," he said.

Made sense I guess. Although a tad on the chubby side at the time, my brother is as strong as anyone I've ever met; and he really, I mean really, can put in a day's work. I just made sure that the team remained well fueled and laughing—a happy worker is a something-or-other worker! Well, rather smiles than tears.

So there we both were, and although it was pretty early, we were both dressed in Bermuda shorts as it was going to be a lot of lifting and an absolute scorcher later. We'd just finished loading the van outside my soon-to-be-old house and had also been hit with the real-ization that we would indeed need another van run after this one. So we hit the road and took off on the penultimate run. Traffic treated us pretty well, and here's something you may not know but there's not an office worker on this entire planet who doesn't love driving vans. The pretend life you can adopt as a builder seems all the more believable in a van. I even stop shaving days in advance to gain extra ruggedness! I buy new clothes and make them all dusty to look the builder type, and I always keep a pencil behind my ear on such days. My brother, an actual builder, finds this hilarious and confusing.

As Radio 2 guided us through the early morning traffic and out onto country lanes, things were looking very rosy indeed. Upon arrival at the new house, the unloading took less than half an hour. We quite literally threw all the boxes in. Unloading is always quicker than loading—not sure why that is, it just is. We chucked as much

9

stuff in the front room as we could fit, jumped back in the van and headed back. An hour and a half later, we were back at the old house for the few final and larger items. My wife, mother-in-law, and Oscar had already set off; it was just us builders remaining to close up shop and get the bulky items loaded. Out came the sofas, fridge freezer, and the cooker; and it's all up and onto the van. My days in suburbia were numbered, and my new coastal village home at the end of nowhere beckoned…living the dream!

We started having problems whilst unplumbing the dishwasher. It just would not un-bloody-plumb, no matter what we tried. Was this the start of things to come? Did an alternative ending start there with the plumb? Probably. In situations like this when you have to make an executive decision in the home, there's only one thing to do. I called my wife.

"Hi, we're having trouble with the dishwasher. Can I just leave it?"

"No, you can't," she said.

"It won't come out the wall."

"Make it come out the wall. Do not leave it."

"I'm leaving the wardrobes."

"No, you're not."

"Do you have any idea how awkward and heavy they are?"

"We need wardrobes, Bertie."

"I'll buy you new ones."

"All right then," she said. "We're off to lunch now at Auntie Di's, call me later, bye."

"Okay, see ya."

I turned to my brother. "Good news, bad news, mate," I said. "Good—we can leave the wardrobes. Bad—it's gonna cost me a new set and we have got to get the dishwasher out."

"Okay," he said. "We'll unscrew it from the fittings and leave the fittings that way all you'll need is some new pipes, and they're ten a penny."

"Sounds like a good idea to me. Let's do that then."

With the van finally full, all we now needed to do was get back to the new house with the last run, unload it, get to the hotel as we weren't completing till the next day, take my brother home the following morning, and then crack on with my new life. Onwards and upwards! I was feeling pretty positive. We grabbed a bucket from KFC, and along with a large jar of my dad's homemade pickled onions for the journey, we were off and running.

At the new house I briefly met with the neighbors, and then my brother and I spent the best part of two hours struggling with a sofa that just would not fit into the living room from the entrance hallway. We tried taking it up the stairs and reversing it back down and in, fat end first, thin end first, legs on, legs off Daniel son, twisting as we walked. It was not going in. That sofa became our nemesis; it was as if it grew every time we picked it up. By the time we decided to take it and leave it upstairs, it was marked, scratched, torn, and covered in blood, sweat, and tears—so to speak. Plus I'd managed to smack a ruddy great big hole in the ceiling. Not the best thing to do. We threw everything else in the house after that as fast as we could and legged it off out of the summer heat wave and into the cooling air-conditioned bar at the hotel. This would be our home for the next few hours.

My phone rang as I was sitting at the bar, feeling pretty pleased with all that I'd achieved today. It was my wife.

"All right, babe?"

"Martin, have you seen the front of the house!" she said sternly.

Hmm, not even a "Hi." This doesn't sound good.

"Yeeeah?" I say, dragging out the "yeah" as I'm trying to think of what it is that I've managed to do.

"Then you'll know that you have knocked down the blinds, that they are hanging diagonally across the front of the window, and everything that you've just shoved in there is now on public display for the current owner, estate agent, and the rest of the world to see. We don't complete until tomorrow. We're not supposed to be in there yet!"

"Yeah, I had a bit of trouble with that blind. It fell off," I said.

"God, you're an idiot at times."

"Hang on a minute. I've busted my nuts off all day doing that. Who cares if anyone sees it?"

"I care, Martin. I care that our new neighbors' first thought is that we are breaking and entering."

"I wouldn't worry about that too much."

"What? Why not? What's happened now?"

"Well, I think I managed to call our new neighbor a dog, inadvertently."

"Oh my good god"—she paused, sighed, paused bit more—"just tell me."

"Well, it wasn't my fault. I pulled up in the van, and this bloke and his wife were standing outside. I said all right, and they said hello. They started asking questions, 'Am I moving in" and how many of us there is and just generally being nosy. I said it's me, you, and the baby. I then asked if they have any kids, thought it would be good for Oscar. They said, 'No, we have dogs.' I then jovially nudged the bloke in a laddish way, and whilst looking and nodding at his wife, I said, 'I've had a few dogs in my time, but it's not stopped me from having a kid.' She seemed to get a bit pissed off, and then they went indoors."

"Oh great, that's just great—good start, Martin, well done," my wife said.

"Can you pop round there and say that I'm usually not that much of an idiot and not to be offended by me or something like that? You're good at that."

"Good at what, Martin? Being normal and not stupid?"

"Yeah.'

"I despair, Martin, I really do. Look, I'll meet you at the hotel," she said in a disappointed sort of sigh.

"Okay, bye," I said spritely. I turn to my brother. "Well, that went well," I said.

A man of few words, he simply replied, "Yeah, I heard. Wanna try this local cider?"

The following morning I awoke to a pounding sensation in my head that can only be compared to that when a gorilla beats its chest.

I was not in good shape. Me and my brother had shared one room; and my wife, baby, and mother-in-law another. The evening before I had indeed said yes to the locally brewed cider offer. Seemed a good idea at the time…. still, onwards and upwards, we've a lot to do today.

After breakfast I realized that the battery on my phone was dead as I had been too drunk to remember to charge it last night. Also I now had nowhere to charge it, and I needed to drive a two-hundred mile round trip to get my brother home. All this whilst waiting on the solicitor to call and advise us on completion, not the best time to be uncontactable. I explained to my wife my error about the phone. It didn't go down overly well, and the added look of disappointment from the mother-in-law added to what was now my building anguish. I called the solicitor on my brother's phone, gave them my wife's contact details, and headed off to get my brother home in the van. Three long hours later, somewhere in southwest London, I get to my brother's flat. I plug the charger into the phone and call my wife.

"We still haven't completed, Martin. All the furniture is on show in the living room because you have knocked the blind down. You do know that we're not supposed to be in there yet, don't you? What if the seller comes round, Martin? Or the estate agent?" It's Martin when I'm in trouble, Bertie when I'm not; and that's just been two Martins, definite trouble. "You never think, you just never think," she continued. "Where are you? You've been gone three hours. I'm stuck homeless with a baby and nowhere to go!"

I had no answer to any of that. I sat there and started feeling very anxious. I needed to get back. Fast. I needed to get back and help or do something. I didn't know what it was I needed to do. I just knew that I needed to get back and do it. Problem was, I didn't know how to get back onto the motorway, let alone get all the way back to the new home. I borrowed my brother's Satnav, which is odd in itself as he can't drive, set the destination, legged it down to the van, and off I went. The Satnav got me totally lost, more lost than I was. What I hadn't realized was that Satnavs don't speak English or

French or Spanish or any recognizable language. They speak Satnav, and I don't. When it says, "Turn right in fifty yards," what does that mean? When's fifty yards? Now? In a bit? In a while? I kept taking the wrong turn and getting stuck in traffic going nowhere, facing the wrong way.

"Turn around, turn around, turn around" was all I heard from this fucking "Crapnav." Anxious and lost in a hot gritty southwest London, I start to fall apart badly. My arms and legs are shaking in the van, and I'm breathing really heavily. I try to tell myself it's okay, try to reassure myself that things are okay.

"Pull it together, Bertie," I say out loud. I look around and all I can see is traffic, traffic, and more traffic. There are roadworks everywhere, and I don't recognize any of the area from the arrival journey. *I have to get back, I have to get back* keeps ringing around in my head. I'm shaking uncontrollably. I start to feel very scared. You know that part of a film that makes you jump? Well, that feeling, that feeling right at that very moment, was constant. With my chest tightening, sweat streaming along my arms and down my forehead, I had to pull over. I had charged my phone briefly at my brother's, so I could make a quick call. I was frantic now and couldn't regain control. I called my wife.

"It's me. I'm lost, panicking, and I don't know what to do. Babe, I'm scared. I'm shaking, I feel sick, and I don't know what to do."

"It's okay," she said. "Everything is fine, you don't need to do anything. Calm, keep calm. We are all fine here. There's nothing for you to worry about. Look, just relax. Get back when you can. Where are you now?"

"Near my brother's, somewhere."

"Call him. Get him to find you."

"Okay, okay, I'll…I'll…ermm…I'll, I'll do that now." I'm stuttering.

"You'll be fine. Just call him."

I don't know how she does it, but the panic subsided. My wife's voice is like a calming wave of beauty and care. It's amazing how the wobble starts to lift just because you know that someone actually gives a shit about you. I sat roadside for a couple of minutes and let the shaking stop.

I called my brother with what power my phone had left. I did my best to act normal. I told him that the Crapnav had sent me down some dead end. He told me to tap "Home" into it, and it would bring me back to his place. My phone then died. But now I had fight; I felt lifted. I knew that I could fight my way through this. I got back to my brother's, and he was waiting outside. He got the Crapnav, tapped in the location, and picked an easy route out of London. It was longer but safer and easier. He and his wife are looking pretty happy; they're about to go out for lunch, and I've hidden the breakdown well. So we say goodbye, and I set off again. This time I seem to understand the SatNav language; I appear to be able to speak it. On the way I start to recognize places from the journey on the way here. Every time I see a place I recognize, I start to feel a bit more relieved, I don't know why. When I see a sign for the M25 motorway, I'm pretty much cured. It's been approximately six long hours since my journey began post-breakfast.

Back at the van rental place, I dropped the van off and gave my wife a call using their office phone.

"Six hours, Bertie?" she says. Turns out my approximation was right. "We haven't completed. The solicitors from our buyer didn't move the funds in time. We're homeless again for the night. Where the hell are you?" *Hell* is as bad as bad language gets from my wife.

"Unbelievable," I said "that solicitor is a massive bag of shit." I tried to redirect her anger from me to the solicitor. That didn't work. And then, wallop, up go the levels of fear and panic. I told her where I was, and she came to pick me up. Together, we decided the best thing to do was to just go into the house. We had the keys. It was not like we'd not been in already, and it was only for one night after all. We'd complete tomorrow, definitely…

Sitting in the back of the car en route to the house, I was crammed in along with a load of house stuff my wife had just bought and Oscar. I could barely get my legs in, and I'd got a box of jars on my lap which, at some stage, would be filled with stuff to be looked at and put on a display shelf.

"We'll claim squatter's rights," I said in a "raise the spirits" kind of way. I hid my internal dread from them. I was falling apart. This entire episode, since dropping my brother off, I think was my first Wobble. If it wasn't the first then it was definitely the one that made me take notice of them. I sat in the back of the car alongside Oscar and watched the backs of my wife's and mother-in-law's head. No one was talking. I just sat there, and I started to feel a change. Away went the fear and panic, and hello, here came the "being swallowed up into a fucking numbness." I found myself not caring. I sat there and stopped caring, thinking, and feeling. I didn't care about anything. Nothing seemed to jump into my mind either. Everyone was quiet, so I just fitted into the external peace and tranquility of the car. Externally, nothing was massively bad: we had the keys, and we were going into the house albeit slightly illegally. I was now back, my brother had probably had a nice lunch, the baby was comfortable and not screaming, all was sort of okay. All except what was going on within me.

We pulled up outside, and we all got out and just walked into our new home. As we went into the house, I clutched my son tight to my chest. I cradled his head—he smelled new. And if beauty were a fragrance, he was that right then, right at that very moment. I wandered up the stairs and stood with him in what would be the new master bedroom. It was spacious and a hideous color, something I would fix in the coming months. It was at this point that I burst into tears. I cried so, so hard. I felt that I needed to draw on Oscar's strength to get out of this predicament. It was embarrassing that I needed to draw on the strength of a six-month-old baby, but I needed to. As his strength filled me, I started to look at our new future, our bright new future in our new home and new town, and I couldn't stop crying. I decided to remain upstairs until someone needed me.

After fifteen minutes or so, my wife walked up to look for me and took Oscar so he could have his dinner, some vegetable mush followed by a chocolate mousse. I used the excuse of hay fever as to why my eyes were red and wet looking. She seemed to buy the excuse and headed back downstairs. I decided that I needed to freshen up, and by jumping into the shower, I could rinse off all the bad feelings and let them wash away down the plug hole. This thought process is absurd, but it seemed totally the right thing to do. *I'll be okay,* I told myself. *It has just been a bit of a stressful day.* I didn't sleep much that night. I started talking to myself over and over about which room needed what doing to it and how I was going to do it and when. I would buy new tools and overalls, of course, then call my brother to help. I thought about the order of the rooms, which was first, second, etc., and when I would start. I wanted to do the garden, but realistically, it would probably be the baby's room first. I felt that I owed him one anyway.

PART 3

ABOUT TWENTY MONTHS BACK, I RECKON

"Good night."

"Yeah, see ya," I turn and say as one guy from the team leaves the office. I then turn to Ron Daly and ask him, "How come that bloke leaves early every night?"

"Only on Fridays," he says.

"What's that got to do with it?"

Ron Daly then bursts into song, "What's tha-at gotta do, gotta do with it! That's wrong, isn't it?"

"Yep. It's what's LOVE. Anyways, why's he gone home"?

"He's a Seven-Day Adventist, you know this," he tells me.

"I don't care if he's Daly Thompson, get him back."

"What?" Ron Daly says as he screws up his face, a look that says, "You fool." "He's not a decathlete, it's a religion. Look, Seven-Day Adventists don't work on Fridays after sunset."

"How does that work?" I say.

"No idea, but sounds like a great religion to me," he says.

"Hold on, it's Thursday today?"

"Yeah he's got dentist."

With everything concerning the move now firmly brushed under the rug, things get back to levels of relative normality. *Hi, my name is Bertie, and I've been Wobble free for x months.* I'm in the office trying to get on with working life and chatting with Ron Daly about random nothingness. It's a pretty average office, very open plan with long lines of desks. We have TV screens absolutely everywhere, plastered all over the walls, telling us absolutely everything we would like to know and we always have some sort of sport on. Some guys have eight screens on their desk, all to themselves—not sure why, never asked. For most of the working day, I live in a glass box that has a cracking view of all the sights the city of London has to offer. There's the London Eye and the O2 arena, formally known as the Millennium Dome. There's Tower Bridge, the Tower of London, and not to mention, the four hundred thousand cranes, each one stabbing London's skyline into a savage submission. Some days I think that the London sky has given up on the fight to be clean and clear and just accepts that the invasion of dirt and smog has won; this day is, however, not today.

I manage a sales trading team, and of course, my door is always open—but only to a select few. If you're on my team and have lost money, tell Ron Daly. If you've made money, tell Ron Daly. If you've lost or gained an account, tell Ron Daly. My door is open to Ron Daly. Ron Daly sits at the top of the row on the sales desk, just in front of my office. This is the desk I run, and I run it at a profit. That's all the bigwigs care about. I do meetings, golf, lunches, the odd conference—that sort of thing. You see, I happen to be rather likeable. I get on with people, and I manage to find that common ground that people have an interest in. I'm a kind of face for the firm. Ron Daly is the engine room. My actual day-to-day job is pretty easy; it wasn't always, but it is now. The main reason for this is that most of all the guys I arrange business with I know and like. We all climbed our ladders together. So by the time we were able to run our own dealing desks, insurance teams, marketing businesses—whatever it was or is—by the time this all came around, we were all in a position to help ourselves by helping each other. We give each other our business, not because it's the best value for money, nor is it because it's great for our business profile. We do it because we all play golf or football or even do pub quizzes together. The whole city works this way; keeping your fingers in the right pies keeps things nice and easy. There's one key point to share here, which is, it is hugely unrewarding where any form of job satisfaction is concerned.

As well as this lacking work effort, I also arrange the night's activities for the team. When I say *the team*, I don't mean the people I work with. I don't like any of them apart from Ron Daly. The team that I mean includes people I like and who like me; these are the people who climbed the ladders. Working in the city, Thursday nights out are an absolute must. I think that the added challenge of making it back into work the next morning all adds to the flavor of the evening. Thursday nights are a morale booster. As I have a level of responsibility at work, I tell myself that it also makes it my responsibility to keep the guys upbeat out of work. Well, only Ron Daly; the others we're out with don't work with me. Ron Daly is a close friend, very close, and as luck would have it, he's very good at his job—very, very good in fact. This helps to make my job very, very easy. We call him Ron Daly because (A) that's his name and (B) it's just one of those names that you have to pronounce both bits. I don't know why, it just is. That's one of the great advantages of being a bloke. When we go out drinking (or anywhere in fact), we go out with Shaolin, Helpful Keith, Smudger, Deckchair, BigFace, and Ron Daly. Nicknames are good; they do a job. Nicknames explain a lot about a person in a very brief format. I'm all for them. People call me Bertie. My full name's Martin Alberts. See? There's a valid link. Shaolin is very acrobatic. Deckchair once did something he shouldn't have on a deckchair. Helpful Keith's helpful. Smudger is a Smith, and BigFace has a big face. When women go out, they go out with Karen, Sarah, and Jane.

That night we meet up at the Windmill Pub. I wouldn't say that it's the best pub in London; it's not the best pub on that street, come to think of it. The beer is well overpriced, and there's a hole in the ceiling big enough to get a family-sized saloon car through. The bar staff are generally aggressive toward us, and the TVs are constantly on flicker mode. Best not go there if you suffer from epilepsy. But it's not full of *city types*, and it's convenient if you use the same train station as me. Not that any of the others do use the same station as me, but if they did, it would be very convenient. We sit around discussing anything that our wives would consider to be "not of any value." We talk and discuss topical events that have no impact on our lives yet keep us entertained. I don't know what we talk about, but I do know that whatever it is, it's stress-free chat.

"Jeremy Spake, Kenneth Williams, Paul O'Grady with Danny La Rue as Hannibal. That's my alternative camp A-Team," Smudger announces. Smudger is as bald as the day he was born, weighs about twenty stone, and looks very menacing—he's not, he just looks it. He's a very kind man who happens to run the tax department in a bank I once worked in.

"Nice," I say in a sarcastic tone. "I'm off to the bar, same again?" Everyone raises their glass with an added grunt. I acknowledge with a nod and suppressed burp. I then get what's required for everyone. Sometimes a grunt is more than enough for a man to uphold a conversation. A few moments later, BigFace—the six-feet, ten-inch, glasses-wearing, ginger-haired global head of complex strategy trading—blurts out, "Cramp Challenge, anyone?" I'm in straightaway. This game is, in my opinion, one of (if not the most) stamina-draining pub contests ever invented by me. The rules are that you must give yourself cramp and then see who can withstand it for the longest time, and we play for money. Myself and BigFace are blessed with the ability to bring on cramp in certain areas of our bodies. I understand that not everyone can do this. Smudger and Ron Daly can't. I opt for my right calf muscle, and BigFace selects his right big toe. This is the test of inner strength, and the fun of watching a man squirm due to self-induced pain never gets old. The bad language and blaspheming ensues, and then three or so minutes later, I collect my winnings. It is then that the landlord, Nigel, comes over.

"I've told ya's before, no gambling in the pub," he says with his Geordie accent. It's a good job one of us went up north once otherwise we'd never know what the fuck he was banging on about.

"We're not gambling," I say.

"Aye, ya's are, Bertie. You've got your trouser leg rolled up. You're playing that stupid cramp game again. BigFace is over there walking his cramp off."

"It's not stupid. It's a test of stamina," I point out.

"No. Gambling. End. Of." Nigel then trudges back behind the bar, back to his area of command. His face is a richness of superiority, oozing with a look of triumph along with the token purple boozy nose. I think the purple nose must be a job specification for landlords of crappy London pubs. If from up north, they also have to wear a football shirt; it's as if they only know nylon as a material.

"If beer be the drink of love, drink on, drink on."

"That's almost Shakespearian," I tell Smudger. "Now shout 'em in."

As a change for that evening, we stay seated in the corner area of the Windmill. Usually we never sit. I've been in pubs that don't even have chairs and never noticed. We are standers; we walk in, get a round in, and stand, sometimes outside. It's a full life.

Smudger returns from the bar with the beers and sits down. "Oi, had a shocker today," he tells us.

"Why? What happened?"

"I was home alone. I'd had a few beers, and so I started to scroll through the channels."

"Wanking?" asked Big Face.

"Well, not at that point. But I was looking for a bit of grot, so I hit the Babechannel, you know the one that you can phone up?"

No one admits to knowing what he's on about; there's just a modest "Hhhmmm" from the group.

Smudge continues, "Well, there's this one bird who looks amazing, and she's really going at it. So I think I'll dial in, you know, just to have a chat. See what she's like."

"I don't think I want to know anymore, Smudge," I say.

"I do, keep going," says BigFace.

"Well, I get through, and you have to select your Babe. So I select this one. Her name's Ruby Red."

"Ginger?" asks BigFace.

"Not really, more a fiery red than an orange. Anyway, I select Ruby."

"First name terms, is it?" I ask.

Smudge ignores me and carries on, "So I select Ruby, and I get told that the Babe I want to speak to is currently chatting to someone else and would I like to hold, select another Babe, or listen in?"

"Listen in to some geezer rattling one off?" asks BigFace with a confused look on his big face. I am also very confused at this moment. Not only about the scenario but also why Smudger wants to tell anyone this.

"Yeah," he says. "You can listen whilst you wait. So that's what I do."

"Whhoooaooao, fucking 'ell, seriously," bellow back the group.

"What? The calls cost a fortune. I want to get my money's worth. Look, anyway, I start to listen in, right? And the geezer on the phone is talking all dirty to Ruby Red."

"I think you should stop now, mate," I say.

Ignoring me again, he continues, "Well, I can't help but think I recognize the voice of the bloke." We're in a stunned silence. We wait...we wait more. Smudge looks uneasy. "Yeah, bit odd, but I think it was my dad?"

"Fuuuuuuck, whooooaaaa, steady!" The group bellow yet again!

The evening winds itself up, and all in all, it's been a decent enough time. I have enjoyed myself; I've laughed and spent time with people I genuinely care about and like. The trouble is, all through the evening, the clouds have been lurking. The Wobble is about to consume me again. It feels dark and cold inside me. As I say goodbye to the stragglers and wander off down Old Broad street toward the train station, I burst into tears. Tears steam from my eyes in what feels like a rampaging facial flood. Each tear dries upon my face only to be replaced by the next. They leave silver streak marks down my cheeks, which I imagine flicker at the sight of car headlights. My eyes throw out tear after tear, and inside I feel numb. I don't feel sad. I'm not crying because I am sad. I don't feel angry either; I just don't feel. There was a time when I had a fire in me, a constant burning rage of

23

a fire. I hated, loved, lived, felt passion. Felt passion about everything whether it be good or bad. I knew things were either shit or amazing; there has never been any middle ground. I was all or nothing. Now I am just nothing. When under the influence of a Wobble, I'm gray, I'm plain, I am a great big blob of nothingness. There is no fire anymore.

As I cry more and more, I realize I can't get on the train, not yet; nor can I go to the station as there's a good chance I'll bump into someone I know, and no one can see me like this. *I am Bertie—a success, tall, and smart. People look up to and admire me.* This is not arrogance; this is just what it is. People don't know that inside I am an eleven-year-old child who can crack because he got stuck in traffic. I decide to wander around the quieter streets of the city for about half an hour or so, behind Liverpool Street station and up toward Shoreditch; there's less of a chance of me bumping into someone I may know in this area at this time of night. I wander around just until the guts of the Wobble can be contained within my facial expressions. I tell myself it is now okay and that the crying will only be on the inside for the rest of this episode. I still feel it there, lurking in the darkness; but as I'm not showing it externally, I head off to the station and jump on the first train I can, which happens to be the last I can. I sit in a mundane green-seated carriage with the few people that made it out and have made the train home. Good news is that as I'm new to this commute, so there's no one I recognize. Something new then arrives in my head. I start to feel differently. *For fucks sake, are the tears and brain numbing not enough?* I start thinking about how I'm feeling, and I have thoughts of hurt, hurting myself. I haven't thought like this before, nor have I actually done any physical damage as such, but the thoughts are now there and have been firmly planted. Then I sleep. I like sleep so much. The sleep stops the feeling, the thinking, and the tears.

I wake up and notice that I'm in the arsehole end of nowhere. I've missed my stop, so I jump off the train at the next stop, which is slap bang in the middle of fuck all.

There are no more trains, no taxi rank, no cashpoint; there's not even a kebab house. I then realize that living where I now live, this is going to be an occupational hazard, and at some stage, I will have to conquer it. I then decide (wrongly it turned out) that I have no other option—other than walking off into the unknown, of course—than to phone home.

"Hi, Babe." Jovial and spritely is my tone.

"What time is it?" Angry and tired is hers.

"Just gone one."

"What are you doing calling?"

"I've missed the stop. I'm in a place called…" I scan and visually hunt for a sign. "Thorpe Leigh on the Naze. There's no trains, taxis, anything. Can you come and pick me up?"

"You do know that we have a baby?" she says.

"Bring him along."

"It's one in the morning, Martin."

"I'm miles away. I think I am anyway."

"Well, I'm afraid that's your fault. Do not call and wake me up again." Then she hangs up.

"Shit. Big fucking shit," I say out loud, talking to no one.

I decide to walk in the direction that the train came into the station from. I am actually pretty pleased with myself for thinking of this. After about forty-five minutes, I recognize a town, realize whereabouts I roughly am, then realize how far away from the house I am. This is literally a hike. I need rambling boots and a big stick for this. Or…a kid's bike? There just so happens to be a bike sitting in a front garden, unchained, with a helmet. It's a no brainer to me. The bike's about three-feet tall and has no gears and no stabilisers. But it's quicker than me walking, and my feet are hurting. I take a picture of the house on my phone so I know where to return the bike, nab the bike in a stealth-like ninja-type fashion, and off I go. From then on, it's a bit of a breeze as most of the journey is flat or downhill, and it takes me about forty-five minutes to get home with only two fall offs and a couple of near ditch misses. I get indoors and collapse onto the sofa of choice for the night. When nights like this happen,

I am pre-warned not to come to bed as I usually "smell like a stale tramp." My eyes close, sticky and sore from the tears and the wind, too, I guess. Before I know it, I'm getting up and getting ready, ready to do it all again.

I get into work the following morning just a smidge late, and Ron Daly points this out to me with a hilarious "Good afternoon." He then tells me that my wife has called and that the car has been stolen. Nice. I call home.

"Hi."

"Bertie, the car's been stolen. Why isn't your phone on?"

"No, it hasn't. I took it to the station, and my battery died."

"What is it with you and phone batteries? Why take my car? Why take a car? The station is a ten-minute walk from our house."

"I had to go to a different station."

"I've called the police," she says.

"Arrgh man alive, what did you do that for?"

"Because I thought the car was stolen. Why did you go to another station? Why didn't you take your car?"

At this point I have no options. And this is where I fess up and remain the child in the grown-up's body. "I had to return a kid's bike I borrowed last night to get home. It wouldn't fit in my car."

"You stole a child's bike?"

"No, I borrowed it. I took it back. Anyway, technically, you're partly to blame."

"How exactly?"

"Cos you wouldn't pick me up."

"Unbelievable. You really are amazing at times. So, Mr. Amazing, how do I get Oscar to baby massage today?"

"Ohhh I dunno, use my car, take a taxi?"

"The baby seat is in the car you took, wherever that is."

"Well, what was I supposed to do? Keep the bike?"

"Sometimes, Martin, you really are an idiot. The police are here. I have to go."

"Don't tell them I stole—I mean, borrowed—the bike."

"Bye, Martin."

"Don't tell them." I plead this final cry for help as the phone goes dead.

Good start to the day, I say to myself. I then get the runner to go and grab some breakfast for everyone. The runner is usually a young person who works on the desk. All the new ones are called runners as they run about for you; I was one once. This runner will probably be in my office one day. He's a bright lad and seems to care about work; he doesn't go drinking, opts for the gym instead. I was like that once, minus the gym part. Actually, I was a tad more in your face. When I was a runner, one of the senior guys who was particularly brash sent me out. He said, and I quote, "Go and get coffees for the desk and get yourself something." To be flash, he gave me a fifty-pound note. When I came back from the errand, I popped the coffees down and gave him back his change. It was exactly two quid. He looked at me then at the two quid and then back at me. He said, "What the fuck is that?" I told him it was his change. He then questioned me as to why coffees had just cost him forty-eight quid. So I said to him, "You said 'Get yourself something,' so I bought a jacket." The rest of the desk all laughed, and to be fair on the guy, he took it really well, all in good fun. But then, he didn't really have much of a choice.

Our runner comes back twenty minutes or so later with coffees plus sausage and egg rolls for the team. Sausage and egg, runny yolk with brown sauce, you can't whack it. That's the hangover cure of choice for me, and over the years, I have introduced it to the team. Apart from the Seven Day Adventist—he's a vegetarian. He gets hash browns and/or toast.

I'm loaded with meetings up until lunch, and seeing as it's Friday and most of the city of London is also hung over, I'll be off to the Windmill for a livener come 12:30 PM, along with most. First things first though, I need to get these meetings out the way. First one sees me along with a few from the floor gathered into a room where some bloke's head pops up on a big screen. He tells us all what the aim of the firm is for the next quarter and how he plans to approach the market with an interest in reducing our risk position and raising current value. All sounds very clever and means nothing to most. The thing about what I actually do is that it makes no sense but makes perfect sense at the same time. Reassurance is what people are after. If they look good and seem to know what's going on, then everyone's happy. This guy on the TV has a high-end groomed look about him. Short smart haircut—jet black, not a gray in sight. He has a dark-blue pin stripe suit, light-blue shirt, hand-woven gold-and-white spotted tie, and of course, the matching tie clip and cuflinks. This man looks the part. For all we know he's embezzling millions in some dodgy offshore account. But he looks good, sounds confident, so everyone's happy. I'm slightly different toward this view as I don't actually give a shit.

Now comes the part of the meeting when I have to speak. I rock back in my chair. Two reasons for this. First, it gives the impression that I'm relaxed, confident, and know what I'm doing. Second, the further back I am, the less chance they can smell the booze from last night. The gray-suited gray-haired tired-looking people from the floor all stare at me. One of them has thrown on a cheeky bow tie today! I think to myself, *It's amazing what wives will do to their husbands.* So as I say, I rock back and tell them about all my meetings that I have lined up, and if there's any additional information they require, they need to speak to Ron Daly—who, unfortunately, couldn't make the meeting as he's too busy with the reduction of the firm's risk exposure. They nod and smile. I smile back, and Bertie has successfully sailed through another meeting whilst knowing not a lot. As James once said, "You can't tell how much suffering is on a face that's always smiling."

Three hours and two meetings later, I'm back at my desk. I grab a Resolve, some chewing gum, and check in with Ron Daly.

"Bloody hell, Bertie, my phone's not stopped with shitty requests about poxy risk positions."

"Oh really? Strange. Sorry mate, I'm straight off for another meeting. Catch up at lunch. Smudger's in the Mill from twelve."

"Call your wife," Ron Daly tells me.

"Will do."

I avoid the desk up till lunch time and head off out. I catch BigFace and Smudger—who, I think, may well have claimed squatters rights—at the bar in the Windmill. Smudger looks awful and still has the same clothes on from last night.

"You all right, Smudge?"

"Getting there, mate. I had to claim squatters rights last night. I kipped here."

"You been to work?"

"Nah, conferences all morning. They're not going to miss me."

"Nice. Right, shout 'em up. Ron Daly's on his way. I'm gonna pop some tunes on," I say in my street, "down with the kid's" voice.

As I wander back over from the juke box, Smudger and Ron Daly, who's just arrived, are talking to BigFace. I sing along to the tune of Chicago—"If you leave me now, you take away the biggest part of me... Oooh, oooh, oh, baby, please don't go."

"You listen to some shit," says Smudger.

"What's wrong with this? Big in its day. Where did you go last night, BigFace? Shot off a tad early," I inquire.

He sighs heavily and then starts to reveal what happened to him last night. "Have this for bad luck," he starts. "A couple of weeks back I crashed into some bloke on the A406. His car wasn't too bad, but mine was a lot worse."

"Your car's a shit tip anyway," Smudger points out.

"I know that, thanks," says BigFace before continuing. "So I said to the guy who I hit, 'Let me know how much the damage is and I'll pay cash rather than claim on insurance for the damages.' That part all went okay. It wasn't massively expensive, and the guy was a right honest John, didn't try to sting me. But when I took my car to the garage, they wanted fifteen-hundred quid. The car's probably only worth about five hundred."

"More like fifty," says Smudger with a firm nod, correcting BigFace's valuation.

"Nice, thanks again. Anyway, I was chatting with my brother-in-law about the situation and, him being a tad dodgy, came up with a solution. He'll steal the car. That way I'll get some insurance back from the theft and I won't have to fork out for the work."

"That's a shit idea," Smudger says, being as helpful as ever; but he has a point, it is a shit idea.

"Yeah, I know that now, but thanks again for the continued input," BigFace continues. "So the plan was wait until around two AM, drive the old wreck into the nearby supermarket car park, leave the keys in the ignition, and walk off. He'll then take the car, burn it out or do whatever they do, and bring back the keys at a later date."

"My god, that is a super shit idea. You are an idiot," says Smudger.

"Yeah, all right, Smudge, we all know how you feel about the idea," I say.

"So"—BigFace sighs and carries on—"I left you lot last night, went home, and waited until about two AM, and took off. But how's my luck? I get to the supermarket car park. It's dark and pretty quiet—a few bakers and a few vans about but no one official looking. The car just about makes the journey, and I get to where I'm supposed to leave it when all of a sudden, these lights spring on me and someone shouts, 'Cut.' They were filming a fucking advert for the supermarket! There were people there all dressed up as bakers and butchers, delivery people and stuff like that. And I've just rolled straight through the middle of the set! I can hardly do an insurance scam now, not after being on tele." BigFace looks really gutted; he stares down at his feet, shaking his head.

Me, Ron Daly, and Smudger say nothing, not a word. We can't. We're too busy laughing at him. BigFace is inconsolable. He's taking this badly, and our laughing would appear to not be of any help.

"That's got to be the... I don't know what that's got to be. That's just brilliant, brilliant," I say. Then Neal Sedaka bursts out of the jukebox, and BigFace groans a bit more.

My wife then calls me to announce that I have been fined £150 and that I have to report tomorrow morning at the police station with identification where I will pay said fine and receive a verbal warning for wasting police time. I think to myself that next time I'll keep the bloody bike.

PART 4

TEN MONTHS AGO

Is it possible that the stupid incidents that follow me around in life are a break from the dread within my own head? These apparent trivial or ridiculous moments are, in fact, what keeps me going; these little breakouts are fun. Well, they are usually fun at first but tend to end badly, like getting thrown out of clubs. Sometimes sitting in a bar with the guys talking about random crap is all I need to break away from the fear of normality and being alone. I find that I am torn between never wanting to actually see people and then seeing people so that I act "normal" and am not bursting into tears but then going overboard on excitement.

One of my less-offensive vices is that I like sweets; I like them a lot. Not chocolate bars as such, more chews, jellies, anything that can fit in my mouth whole. I like to pop a sweet in and not have to hold anything like a bag of crisps or a piece of cake. Because of this, I usually have sweets on or around me at all times. If you were to look in my drawer at the office, you may well be forgiven for thinking that Willy Wonka had been mugged. Tonight we're going out to a club, not that I really want to. But I know it'll be good for me to go, to get out, and the choice of sweet is toffee chocolate éclairs. These little bad boys are hard toffee with a soft chocolate center. They are individual, approximately the size of a large grape, and are currently all in a white paper bag in my pocket for easy access. I've unwrapped them from their individual wrappers because I like to grab at them quickly and pop one in my gob without having to faff about with the wrappers. Well, there is that reason, but more importantly, I don't want to be spotted by the people I am out with eating my sweets 'cos then I'd have to share. This way they're all ready for speedy dispatch.

The planned evening is to celebrate my sister's birthday. My wife and I, along with a large group of people whom I don't like, are all going to a "Skool Disco"—which means I have to dress up like a dick and the only white shirts I have, have cufflinks, which is not very schoolboy. Turns out though that when my wife puts on her uniform, she looks great! Considering seven weeks back, she delivered our second child, Lazlo, she looks amazing. Probably a tad worrying that I enjoy the view a bit too much, but hey ho, it's all in good nature, I think? I mean, is it right that people are dressing up in school uniforms to get fiercely drunk and dance in a sweaty room to songs from the 1980s? Look, I don't know if it's right, wrong, or very wrong; but it should be fun, and that's what I keep telling myself. Albeit I am with a bunch of people I dislike.

I have no idea how my sister and her girlfriends managed to pick such a bunch of arseholes to be their boyfriends, but they hit the home run on arseholes. Serious arseholes. There's this one guy, Angus, easily the greatest man on the planet in his own head. A big fat fucker who's happy to be rude to every man and his dog at all times for the sole reason that everyone is beneath him. There's also Todd (that's my sister's fellow). He's going to be a writer and does *crazy dancing* for the benefit of the room. He does this, I think, because he can't dance for shit and wants to be ironic. I'm no Michael Jackson, but how hard can it be to tap a foot and clap now and then?

Then there's Leon, a totally boring pot-headed nob. I don't see the draw of weed, not after the age of sixteen anyway. Not when you might actually like to talk to people, get out of the house, and turn off the Discovery channel. Leon smokes some type of high-grade weed, so on the basis of this, he's the cool one of the group. In my humble opinion he's a borderline vegetable. Conversation with him goes as far as "Hi, what have you been up to?"

"Not much. Smoking some new bad shit, you know."

And there's Todd's brother. I think he's called Ben, but I'm not 100 percent sure because he talks only to Angus. I guess this is due to some group hierarchy and Ben's total worship of arseholes. I'm guessing Ben, if that is his name, is on the cusp of being in the select group. Problem is, Ben's younger than the others, his big brother ridicules him at any opportunity and he doesn't have a girlfriend. When Ben gets a girlfriend (if he gets one), the girls already in the group will not accept her and, therefore, will be bitchy toward her. Then the girlfriend and Ben will either leave the group altogether, or Ben will stay, be single, and will be continually ridiculed. I don't know why. I fail to understand why. It's just how they are. I don't really give a toss either.

Me and my wife drive over to my sister's place in a ridiculously expensive part of West London where we all meet up. My sister's what I call a London trendy—ergo her flat is an "apartment" and she loves "the arts." Realistically, she's a short, lovable, and feisty little sister from a council estate who's done well for herself. Upon arrival, I see that Todd's already doing his crazy dance moves in the flat. I start to mingle and drink some overpriced exotic beers from around the world. I'm not allowed to drink stout in my sister's apartment. Ideally, she'd not have me drink stout at all. My sister says it's for old men who sit around and play dominoes in stinky old pubs. In truth, I wouldn't mind sitting around playing dominoes; but tonight is her night, her rules, and I'm here. So this is me doing my bit. Our brother just said no. Well, what he actually said was "I'm not going out with you and your arsehole mates." Like I've mentioned, he's a man of few words.

We've all been allocated VIP tickets by my sister for the disco tonight; this is just so that we don't have to queue because queuing is *not cool*, apparently. I don't really mind either way, but what I do mind is that we all have to get there late. The beer in the apartment is running out, but we can't leave for the disco because we don't want to get there too early. The clubs open, the bars inside there will be open, the queue at the bar will be small, but again it's *not cool* to be on time. We hang around for another hour listening to some new band that are just about to storm onto the scene. Next big thing, so my sister says. I dared not say that they are no match for Chicago or Toto for that matter.

After what feels like a lifetime, the taxis turn up. My wife gets into the girls' car, so I have to go with the boys. My wife seems to think that I'll have more of a fun time with the guys rather than being squeezed up against a load of women dressed as schoolgirls. I then realize the extra good news: I'm sharing a taxi with Angus. The majority of the journey consists of Angus being nasty to the driver. He boasts about how little the taxi driver earns and the hours he has to do because Angus himself is raking it in for doing very little. Then, just five minutes into the journey, Angus declares to us that he needs to get to the club so he can have his "fifth shit of the day." I won't be shaking his hand at the end of the night. Seeing that Angus is in the car, so is Ben, who just so happens to think that Angus's latest comment is great, surprisingly. Ben retorts, "Whoa, good effort." Personally, I think he should see a doctor.

When the cab pulls up outside the club and we get out, I look to see the crowd of people queuing; this looks nothing short of a fetish party to me. Angus darts off immediately. I forgot to mention he's tighter than a fish's arsehole. Ben just stands there and looks despondent, waiting for instructions—that or a handout. This means that I pay the cab fare. We meet up with the girls at the entrance and head to the main door with our special tickets. Once inside I cling to my wife like a wino to a bottle of methylated spirits. What I don't want to happen is that I get separated and end up with the crazy dance gang. The club itself is quite nice in fact which surprise me. I haven't been to a club on purpose for a night of clubbing in about ten years, possibly longer. But this one—albeit we're all dressed as fetish-loving schoolboys and schoolgirls—is a nice place, and what surprises me even more is I start to have a good time. The building was once a cinema and still has a similar setup. As you walk in, there are bars to the left and right where there were once popcorn and sweet sellers. The main area has a large dance floor at the base of what was once the front seats, and the DJ peers over all comers that dance before him. He is up in a booth that was once the movie screen. Then up behind the dance floor is basically a viewing gallery where the higher-situated movie seats would have been to watch a film. They slope up and away into darkness only to be seen in a split second when the lights flash.

I get myself well settled in and find a spot just near the popcorn bar with a standing table that becomes "base camp" for all of us for all the night to come. Now the beers will need to start to flow; this will only happen depending on how often I go to the bar. My sister's not paying as it's her birthday. My wife's not paying because she's out with me and driving. Angus isn't paying—"Not at these prices"— and not with his illness that provokes him from putting his hand in his pocket. Honestly, that bloke, I bet he doesn't like breathing because he has to give up air. Ben's skint, Todd's off crazy dancing, and I'm thirsty. After a while of being in there, I'd managed to have had a skinful of overpriced bottled beer and a couple of shots. I was really enjoying myself. I even spoke to Todd about normal things and laughed a little.

Like most nightclubs, this one starts to get pretty hot—nice and hot and sticky and hot and dry and hot. I start to feel like I'm melting, and then I realize that I actually am, of sorts. The toffee chocolate éclairs!? I can feel a warm sticky squishiness in my back pocket. I turn to check my trousers, and I spot that I now have a large dark greasy patch which, when squeezed, resembles the feeling of a waterbed. I dash off to the mens room, bust into the toilet cubicle, and whip down my slacks to look at the mass of chocolate and toffee goo. I don't take my trousers fully off as this would mean removing my shoes, and you should never wander shoeless in any male public toilet. The goo is about the size of a fist, and it's nesting in my back pocket. The greasy, sticky, damp patch has spread and is covering both bum cheeks of the trousers. *Great, fucking great,* I think to myself. *What to do now?* I start to dig and scoop out the goo with my hand from the back pocket of my trousers, which are sitting around my ankles. Then there's a knock on the door.

"Excuse me, sir, can you open the door, please?"

"What? Hang on, mate."

"Sir, open the door now, or I'll be forced to kick it in."

"What? Hold on, I'll be done in a minute," I say.

"Sir, this is security. You've been in there a while. If I have reason to believe you're doing something you should not be doing in there, I'm going to kick the door open."

"Hold on, hold on," I scream back in a panic.

"Stand back" is the last thing I hear. *Boom!* He kicks the fucking door in. He then stands there looking in at me. And as he looks in, there I am. I'm crouched over the toilet to avoid the door hitting me, bent over in a type of squatting position with my hand held out in front of me, which is clutching a mass of brown goo that also happens to be dripping through my fingers and onto the floor. There's a brief moment of silence as he just stares at me.

"That's disgusting. You disgust me," he says this with a screwed-up angry face, emphasizing his disgust. He looks mean, bordering sick, bordering violent.

I look at the goo sitting in my hand. I then look at him, back at the goo, then back at him, all this whilst still in a sort of squat position and shaking my head. "Nah, nah, nah, it's not that," I say. But the security guy is having none of it. He interrupts me.

"Clean up and get out. That's filthy," he shouts. "I'll be waiting outside, and I'll be escorting you off the premises. Sick, you're sick. You've got two minutes, hurry up." He says this to me whilst shaking his head. He then storms out of the toilets. I'm now left there, and in all honesty, I'm a tad stunned at what's just happened. I think I'm being thrown out of a nightclub for the sole reason of playing in and with what he thinks is my own shit! Nice. I scrape the goo from my hands and flush away as much as I can. I was going to attempt to hand-wash and dry my trousers, but there doesn't seem to be much point now.

I leave the cubicle, and as promised, Mr. Security is waiting for me just outside the main toilet door.

"Right, ready? I'm not touching you, but you're leaving right now, this way," he informs me and waves me forward.

"Look, mate," I say, "it's not what you think. Granted it looks bad, but the mess was from melted sweets. I'm hardly likely to shit myself, am I? I'm not six months old."

His expression doesn't change though. He just keeps marching forward whilst keeping me in front of him and guiding me to the exit. I then realize that he can't actually hear me over the music plus he's got a headset on and he's talking into it. I assume my case is closed and judgment has been made.

A couple of minutes later I'm dumped out onto the curb, alone, dressed as a schoolboy, and a little disappointed with the night to say the least. I stand there trying to assess the situation. I'm pretty sure that mobile phones won't be working in the club, but always the optimist, I call my wife. "The number you have dialed is unavailable. Please try again later." Shit!

As I stand there and assess, I notice that there's an encroaching smell surrounding me. and it's nasty, really rife. It smells just like that smell when you walk past the back of a rubbish truck on a really hot day—sweet, sickly, shitty, and grubby with a hint of sweat. I turn my head to try to locate this horrendous odor, and I see a short, drunk, homeless tramp standing within about three inches of me. Good job he's not any closer, I don't think I could take the aroma! I have the impression that this gentleman of the street has never heard of personal space. I back up a bit. He's got one shoe where his foot hangs out the front and one shoe where is foot hangs out the side. He's donning a yellowy-gray mac whilst leaning on one crutch, for sympathy I'm guessing. He has a green "Sunny Days Holiday" visor cap thing and some filthy dark trousers that hang down like some sort of poor man's MC Hammer tribute act. We're both standing there, staring—

my face a tad disgruntled, his face a tad dirt ridden. Then he says all chirpily, "Got any cash, mate?"

"Cash? Fuck me, don't you lot ask for 'just change' anymore?" I say. Granted, I'm in a bit of a bad mood and my response may have been a bit aggressive, but all in all, I feel entitled to have a go at someone; and Mr. Chirpy is here, so why not him?

Mr. Chirpy then turns into Mr. Disgruntled. "No need to get all aggressive. I'm just trying to get by in the world."

"No need to get aggressive? Who are you? A therapist? Look, piss off."

"I bet you wouldn't say that to me if I was a big bloke," he said.

"Bet???" I say. "What the fuck have you got to bet with? Look, piss off, mate. I'm proper not in the mood." He grumbles and slurs something or other and then wanders off to his next victim of nasal assault.

This night has gone from pretty good to really shit within ten minutes. I can't go home and leave my wife in the club. Our car is at my sister's, and she's driving. So I've got no choice. I'll have to wait till someone misses me, realizes I'm not about, finds an area where mobiles can get a signal and then calls me. Meanwhile I send a few text messages to the people inside the club explaining that I'm outside because, through no fault of my own, I've been ejected from the club. Obviously, no one replies. On the plus side, I think, due to us being fashionably late, the club's only open for another couple of hours. And at least it's not freezing or raining. So worst-case scenario, I hang about getting weird stares for a bit. Hammersmith isn't the best place in the world to spend two hours. Well, one hour and thirty-five minutes as it turned out. That's how long it took them to notice I was missing. During this time, I wondered who was buying the beers.

Next morning is the day that we're setting off on a sort of holiday. We're going to stay in my wife's uncle's caravan on a campsite. The kitchen's being replaced at home, so we can't really be there; and my wife thinks it'll be fun to go and live in a caravan for a week. I hate caravans; tents; toilet blocks; boating lakes; foldout beds; mini fridges; gas bottles; portaloos; wellington boots; bonfires; people with socks pulled right up; plastic chairs, knives, forks, plates, cups; toilets the size of shoeboxes; low plastic ceilings; push-up windows on roofs; tents that attach to caravans that aren't tents but called awnings; and anything else related to fucking caravanning. So on that basis, this should be fun. Plus I have to commute for two days from the caravan as I can't get the full week off from work. Blinding!

We're in a little place near our house, about a forty-five minute country-lane drive away. We want to keep an eye on the builders, so technically, it's not that bad an idea. Technically, on paper, it could be all right. It won't be. But technically, on paper, it could be; but it won't be. At the site, the old trampy-looking caravan site owner wanders over to me. "It's 'undred pound for the week," he says with his really deep Suffolk-country accent that makes him sound like an old cider-drinking worzel. "Cash only."

"I've only a fifty on me," I say. "Can we set ourselves up first, and then I'll pop to the cashpoint?"

"Nope."

"Really?" I say with a screwed-up, bemused look. "I mean it's not as if I'm going to run off with a two-ton caravan, is it?"

"Yes, really, money upfront before you get on your plot. We prefer it that way."

"Look, mate, let me just set this pile up, and you can have your cash in an hour. I'm not gonna run off and leave you, am I? Nor am I going to knock you for fifty quid."

"Nope. There's plenty of cash machines in town," he says.

Stubborn git, I think to myself. "I'll write you a cheque. I've got the book in the car."

"Nope."

"How about I write you a cheque for two-hundred quid? You can have it as a holding deposit, and if I don't pay cash after we've set up, you can keep the cheque—that's fair."

"Nope. Cash is only what we take 'ere."

This man is pissing me off. Technically, he works in the hospitality industry. He's about as hospitable as a bull in the Pamplona run.

"Arrrgh, this is total bollommm—" My wife sticks her hand over my mouth and stops me speaking mid flow.

"Bertie, go to the cashpoint and get the man his money. You could have been there and back by now if you weren't being so difficult."

Difficult? Me? And since when has it been his money? I strop off to the cashpoint. After I pay, we—well, I—set up the caravan and the tenty thing that hangs on the side. We unpack all the new gizmos we've bought that all seem to fold up. And then, we sit. We sit in our little tent attached to the side of the caravan. Oscar rolls about a bit and eats a few stones, bugs, whatever he can find. Lazlo sleeps and we just sit. I look around and notice that everyone just sits. Oh, and then after a while, I find out that you have to talk to everyone you see at every opportunity. I think this must be some sort of caravanner's rule: if you walk past a man or woman (but not a child) on the way to anywhere, you have to stop and chat.

"Towing?" One caravanner says to me as I venture up and out of my seat and into the public area with Oscar in the buggy.

"Sorry?" Out comes my screwed-up, bemused face again.

"You towing?" he says as he points to the caravan we're staying in. By this I think he means, Do I lug this heap up and down the country on the back of a family estate car?

"No, we're just borrowing our friend's van for a week," I say.

"Hmmm," he replies. He says this with a disapproving "You're not as good as me" look on his face. "Yeah, we tow. We came down from—"

"I don't care, mate. Bye." I cut him off and wander off. Now this may not seem massively friendly, but I'm stressed. I'm tired and I've gotta get up at 4:30 AM. Oscar has started screaming in the buggy, I need to order a takeaway, and I want to get a pint in before my face drops away from my head as a result of all the times I keep rubbing it with both my hands. Apparently, that's a sign of distress in itself.

I push Oscar up to the pub and have a swifty where Oscar settles into snooze mode. Meanwhile I've ordered the Chinese that will be ready in five minutes—how do they make it so fast? My wife is back at the van with Lazlo making it all "homely and all lovely." I think you can make it homely by sticking a flat-screen TV and Sky Sports in there. It's of no surprise that I struggle with the whole "being positive" thing. I know that. It's something I am aware of, but at the same time, it's something that I don't seem to be able to snap out of.

About an hour or so passes by. We've finished our dinner. We bathed the boys in the sink, and they're in their bed, which is also our bed. We both sit outside chatting with a beer. It's nice. I try to think it's nice. *No, this is nice,* I decide. I tell myself this is nice. It's not too cold, there are no distractions, and we're both just chatting about the week ahead. My wife says that it's a shame I have to go to work for the next two days but we'll have a nice time anyway and that it'll be better when I'm around for the whole day. The nicey bit of the day comes to a close, and we head off to bed. I feel calm and relaxed; I've not felt this for some time.

The morning arrives, and the nicety of last night is a far memory. The shower in the caravan does work, but we're not allowed to use it because my wife's uncle said so. Therefore, I have to go over to the shower block. Now as I am not yet a caravanning expert, I'm lacking in the relevant knowledge on how to wash in "the block" and what it is I need. I take a towel, shower gel, toothbrush, toothpaste, and some sculpting mud for my hair. Turns out this is not enough equipment. I realize I am unequipped after about two seconds of leaving the van. I will also need flip-flops or some kind of footwear. There's gravel everywhere, and I'm Billy Barefoot for the journey into the block.

When in the block—a square cold, concrete pink block—I see that there are some fluids on the floor, some bleach, some not bleach. Whatever the "not bleach" is, you don't want to be Billy Barefoot in it. I opt for the shower with the curtain as opposed to the one without, but seeing as it's 4:30 AM, I don't think many people will be bursting in on me. The shower takes an age to warm up, so I have no choice but to brave the cold water in the hope that in any second the heat'll kick in. That doesn't happen. All that does happen is that the shower curtain chases me around the cubicle like some crazed ghost. It clings onto me like an old lady who just met Daniel O'Donnell. I can't take the cold for too long, so I get out and grab my towel. It is then, just behind where I hang my towel, I see a small box: "Insert 50p here for hot water." Nice. I'll remember that for tomorrow along with the flip-flops, I tell myself. I dry off and then I realize another thing I need: a change of clothes. You can't put the T-shirt and shorts back on that you've just slept in; that's not allowed. Blazin Mayes, an old friend once said, "Dirty clothes on a clean body is not allowed"; and I do what I am told sometimes, and this is one of the times. I have to wander back with just a towel wrapped around me, back over the gravel whilst freezing my little nuts off. My suit and shirt are hanging outside in the tent attachment part of the caravan, so that's nice and cold too. I put them on and think gladly, sort of, that at least no one's around to see me getting dressed peering through the plastic window. I kiss my wife, Oscar, and Lazlo goodbye; jump in the car; put the heating up full blast; and head off to the station.

At the station I realize my regular train pass is at home, so I approach the ticket office to get a temporary pass or an add-on or whatever it is that they do. I am then told that I will have to buy a return ticket and then fill out a form and claim back the cost of the fare at a later time. I point out to the employee that when I bought my season ticket, they take down all my particulars; ergo, they know that I have a season ticket. They know who I am and where I live, so why can't they just give me a temporary pass? He stares at me blankly. I find that the people who work on, near, or with trains are particularly frustrating.

"Okay, just a return to Liverpool Street then, please," I say.

"That'll be £57, please."

I almost choke. "Liverpool Street in London, not Liverpool the city."

"Yes, it's £57, peak-time price I'm afraid," he says. I don't know why he's afraid.

"Peak time? It's 5:30 in the morning. What's peak about the 5:38 train?"

"Sir, it's any time before nine AM, I'm afraid."

"Okay, so what do I get for fifty-seven quid?"

"Sorry, sir?" he says looking confused.

"Well, for example, for fifty-seven quid I could drive to work and back. I would get my own seat, listen to the radio or a CD of my choice, not have to stop every ten minutes, and still have enough money for a coffee or a bagel or whatever. So…what do I get FOR FIFTY-SEVEN FUCKING QUID!!!! Apart from totally shafted that is."

He looks a bit uneasy and slightly shaken by my rant. "Sooooo do you want the ticket, sir?" he asks.

"Love one, that'll be great. Thanks, thanks very much. Have a great day."

He then smiles and cheers up immediately, missing all my sarcasm. He prints off my orange-and-yellow fifty-seven-pound cards—I get two—and hands them to me. "Thanks to you too, sir. Enjoy your journey," he says.

Shocking morning all in all, and it's not even 7:00 AM. I need to do something. I need to do something to cheer myself up; I think I do. I get to Liverpool Street station, jump off the train, and walk up the exit stairs and onto the city pavements. I see that there's a man setting up a market stall getting ready to sell these walking, barking fluffy robot dogs. As I walk up toward the stand, one of the dogs is yapping away and looking all cute and cuddly just out in front of me on the pavement. I can't help myself from doing this, I can't. I kick it under an oncoming bus. I caught it really well, just on the underbelly between the legs—kept it low but fiercely struck. I give the bloke a fiver for the dog and then continue on the way to the office. *There,* I think, *that's released some tension. Let the day begin.*

PART 5

FIVE MONTHS AGO,
NEARLY CHRISTMAS

A bad day, a very bad day, has hit me. The Wobbles seem to be more regular and more intense these days; they last longer and I seem to slip deeper into myself. I had previously decided that I needed a change, so I looked for a new job and got one. I moved in the summer to a new firm, and I now work with and for some pretty nice and normal people. They don't want change; they like things as they are, and I now struggle to fill my day. The work is easy, far too easy, and very simple to improve things. This firm should not be paying me what they are to do what I am now doing. This lack of required concentration I'm sure is adding to the impact of the Wobbles.

On most evenings, as I walk to the train station on my way home, I cry. When in the office, I wander off and away from my team daily. I go up out onto the fire escape stairways for an escape and mini breakdowns. The fire escape becomes an ally. I wonder where I would be physically without it. If things manage to get too intense, I go upstairs via the fire escape to one of the empty offices above and just stare out the window, looking down at anything and nothing. I can't tell you what it is I see or what it is I feel unless I am able to say that what I see and feel is nothing itself.

I think I hate this new firm. I think that I should just knock everyone out every day, but then at the same time, all my passion and fight is being sucked out of me. Instead of being the confident man I was, now I just appear to muddle through and trudge on. I now fit in with all the gray faces. I moved jobs for a new challenge after receiving a call from a headhunter to head up a new desk at a new firm, and I thought the fresh move would be good; plus the sweetener of more money always adds to the decision. About a month or so after I moved, the financial markets collapsed. This meant two things:

1. We can't make money because we can't take risks; therefore, we do little (if any) work.
2. I'm lucky to have a job, let alone a shit one. If I start making waves or piss off the wrong person, it's pretty easy for them to say, "Bye-bye, pack your stuff and fuck off." I've seen that happen before.

I have to fit in; so I have to look busy, sound productive, and be positive, which, as it happens, is a skill that I have developed over time. I've hidden these Wobbles from my immediate family and friends, so doing the same to new colleagues and other strangers should be a fucking breeze. One of the keys to looking busy is meetings. Get in them, get them booked in your diary, get a chart stuck up in your office, and throw up meeting after meeting on it. It doesn't matter who sees the planner on the wall, nor does it matter how they interpret it. When I say to anyone, "Can't talk now, got a meeting," no one has ever said to me, "Oh yeah, what meeting are you going to?" or "Who is it with?" People just assume that you're busy and important. And that's fine with me.

My first actual meeting on this particularly bad day was one with my brother, in the pub, for a long lunch. This morning I cried on the way to the office rather than the way home; hopefully, that's it for the day. The last thing I really need are tears on the way in and out of work. I've kept it together all morning, post the tears, and now I'm going to see my brother. I need to keep it together. I can't crack up on him although all I want to do is to grab him, hold him close, and sob my fucking eyes out all over him; but I can't let that happen. On my way down to meet him for lunch, I manage to hide all my shit inside somewhere deep down, and as I wander into the bar that is just around the corner from my new office, I start smiling. The reason that we've both met up today is to talk about what we're going to do with Dad this year for Christmas.

"I'm taking him Christmas shopping as usual," I say. "But I'm not seeing him on the day."

"Okay, I'll try and get over to see him," he says.

So now that it's sorted then, I'll take Dad out, buy his presents, buy him a beer and some dinner, and my brother will see him on the day. My sister was going away as per usual, so it was down to us to sort out.

"Beers then. Now that's sorted," I say.

Christmases turned sour for me about fifteen years ago, so it's pretty much always been a tough time since then. Don't get me wrong. Since Oscar was born there's been a great deal of anticipation, hoping that he—and now Lazlo—will have a nice time. And in truth it's more a relief than anything. I can put my efforts into them and not the other two people who made Christmas so shit for so long. This particular Christmas though, this one, however, was a tough one—not the toughest but tough nonetheless. It was the first one where I had decided not to see my dad. I used my kids as an excuse, not that I needed one as I'd put my hours in over the past fifteen years. But this time I also knew, I think I knew, that this would probably be his last. I knew inside, and I was pretty sure that because I knew, I had enough emotional strength to get through it. I'm Bertie; I'll take on my troubles, your troubles, and if you've got friends with troubles, send them over to me too. This may well be one of the roots of my Wobbles. Anyway, it went shit for me at Christmas about fifteen years ago, so since then, I've always dreaded them.

Winston Churchill used to call it "Dark Dog," I think. Unless you've ever had a Wobble, you're unlikely to understand them or hold any empathy for anyone who has had them. I always thought that depression (and that's not what I have by the way, I'm just a bit down that's all) was a made-up illness for self-pitying folk. I thought it was for lazy people who don't want to face up to the world, so instead, they just moan and say that they have something wrong with them just for an excuse. That is what I once thought, not anymore. I was wrong and a prick for thinking that. No longer can I ever think that, not after I spend day after day crying in fire escapes. But still, onwards and upwards. I tell myself, *Keep going. You'll be right, Bertie. It's just a blip that's all.*

I don't think Christmas is the cause of anything bad for me in itself; it just doesn't help anything. But with the added knowing pressure that this year will probably be my dad's last as he continues to drink himself into a wooden box, this is another additional factor and reason for a Wobble. This man, my dad, was once a bit of a dancer, a cricketer, a butcher, always social, got on with everyone, and was reasonably confident. He was never someone I would go to for advice (more the other way, in fact), but he was a nice person. A much nicer person than I am. Now though he just shakes and cries when he's around me, but it's a nervous sort of shake and cry not a "feeling upset" shake and cry. It's a tad odd.

My brother and I sit back and chat that afternoon for quite a while. We speak about our dad and his antics—some good, most bad, and most also being financially damning to me. We had both agreed—or rather concluded to—that at one point in his life, our dad had managed to turn into a Bertie-life wrecking ball. He'd lost his job as a glazier for the council after being caught drinking whilst at work. He had thought it was a good idea to leave his two-ton yellow van outside a pub situated ten seconds away from the management offices whilst he was inside said pub for a good few hours. He actually wonders how they managed to spot him and puts it down to bad luck. Shortly after this episode, my mum sold his house and left him with legal fees for the divorce—a divorce that she initiated by having an affair—and of course, I then had to pay said fees. I then rehomed my dad just around the corner from where I lived, hoping I could keep an eye out for him and keep him busy. I gave him odd jobs around my ever-developing house. To be fair it was working quite well, at first. He'd pop round, mow the lawn, open the house for the plumbers and builders, and take in deliveries whilst we were out. Sadly, what I didn't realize at the time was that at the same time of him being in the house for the odd jobs, he was working his way through an entire cabinet of spirits from around the world.

After we had finally finished all the decorating on this house, we sold it, sold it whilst the paint was still drying. Then one day, whilst in the middle of boxing up our life to move to the new village home, my wife started on the kitchen. My wife was packing all the kitchen stuff up one drawer at a time and had got round to the cabinet that housed all the spirits. Well, it was where all the spirits were supposed to be. This is when my wife realized that during his trips over to mow the lawn and so on, Dad had managed to bomb through three different types of vodka, all unopened when he had found them. Two were gifts for my wife from friends in Hungary and Norway. As well as that he'd necked a bottle of sherry, two bottles of brandy, a bottle of whisky, Baileys, and some Hardys Bristol Cream!! And being the mastermind that he is, he'd just popped all the empty bottles back in the cabinet. I'm guessing so that we wouldn't notice. And we didn't. Well, not until we moved house that is.

I got home that day from work to see my wife sitting down and looking very disappointed whilst holding Oscar on her lap. She was ready to break the news of her findings to me. What do you say? What do you say to the woman who's helped you to support your father through all the shit he's been through and, in turn, he put us through shit? What do you say to your wife when she tells you that your dad has stolen from us? Sadly, this episode wasn't the worst of it. When I moved Dad to live closer to us, I had put him in a flat I owned. I had planned to let it to tenants but needs must prevail. He needed somewhere to live, and I needed to keep an eye on him. But whilst Dad was living in my flat, he managed to do his best to destroy the place.

It was on one particular morning that I'd just returned from the shops and was standing just on the cusp of my drive when I saw Dad walking toward me looking a tad worried. He then informed me that he was in a "bit of trouble."

"What now?" I asked. "Who with?" He told me he was in trouble with me. I said sternly, "'What the fuck have you done this time, Dad?" And he stood there and told me he'd had a fire. After passing out drunk of course and leaving the cooker hob on. Albeit he never said drunk; he said he just fell asleep. I pretty much went ballistic at this point. I told him that after everything he had done and all of what I had done that I was at a loss as to where to go next with him. He'd lost his job, his home, and was in monumental amounts of debt. I had rehomed him, given him a job (of sorts), and paid off the debts, and all he had to do was to stay out of trouble. Instead he had tried to burn down my fucking flat. Not to mention the car I once owned, which he borrowed and wrote off. He failed time after time to understand the strain that he managed to put on me and those who cared about me. All I ever, ever said to people about him was usually bad stuff.

After that brief and yet fulfilling meeting with my dad, I remember going back indoors. My wife is in the kitchen having a coffee, and she offers me one. "Everything okay, babe?" she says. "Just having coffee before we leave to go to Mum and Dad's. Do you want one?"

"Please. I just saw my dad," I say.

"Oh yes, how is he?"

"Not bad, not bad considering he's just torched the flat." Stunned into laughter is how I would describe what happened next. *This man, this sweet-hearted buffoon, is slowly breaking me down,* I think, but at the same time, you have to laugh, I guess.

That coming summer was to be the summer that we moved away, and this then meant that it was going to be the first Christmas that

Dad was going to be alone. He'd never been much of a Christmassy sort, so taking him out shopping beforehand, having lunch, and a beer suited him a lot more than it would, say, being at mine with the in-laws on the big day. He wasn't a massive fan of opening presents, I have no idea why, but then I have no idea why he would sniff his fork before Sunday mealtimes. It's just what he did.

Me and my brother finish up our drinks and chat, and I go back to the office for the rest of the afternoon. I call Dad and tell him where and when to meet me so that we can go Christmas shopping. After about an hour, I wander up to the roof of my building. I'm not crying, and I'm not entirely sure what the reasons are that I go up there.

The "Christmas shopping with my dad" day arrives, and the first signs are not good. I'd left work early, and we had arranged to get together just by Fenchurch Street station. He only needed to get five things, and Fenchurch Street with Bishopsgate alongside it has plenty to offer the man searching for Christmas gifts. I wandered up the City's chilly, rushed, and packed streets to where we had arranged to meet. Dad was waiting for me outside the entrance of Marks & Spencer—he'd probably been there about an hour. Not that I was late, he just would have been early. When I saw him, his hair was white, totally white, and he was really thin. I hadn't seen him for a couple of months. We'd been in touch on the phone, just not met up in person. I was shocked how drastically he had changed since not having me close by anymore. Over these months, he'd managed to turn into a POW camp lookylikey. He was 61 years old but looked 101. I decided that I couldn't drag him round the shops. I didn't think he could walk much further than he already had plus it had just started hammering down with rain. I was scared to shake his hand; I thought it'd snap off as soon as I touched it. My brother had surprisingly met up with us too, so we decided that the best thing to do was to send them both into the nearest Weatherspoons on Bishopsgate. I went off to grab the gifts for my family from my dad. All in all, it took about twenty-five minutes. It didn't matter if the presents were shit; no one expected much from him. I grabbed smellies for the girls, smellies for the boys, clothes for the children, and a rather nice shirt and tie for my good self. Well, if you think I'm doing this and not getting any perks, you're mistaken.

I walked back down Bishopsgate and to the pub to find my dad and brother sitting at one of those raised tables. It's a table that you can sit at with barstools rather than chairs. I like them cos you can dangle your legs. I'm six feet, five inches tall. Dangling my legs stopped when I was about five right up until these chairs/stools came into my life. My brother and dad are not saying much; my dad doesn't like my brother. I don't know why. I fucking love the bloke; I think he's great. But my dad just has very little time for him.

"Right, I'm not wrapping them. You can do that yourself," I say as I drop the presents on the table.

"Oh yeah, that's good. I'll do that. Have you got any paper?"

"Fuck me sideways, Dad. What else do you want? I choose them. I buy them. Would you rather I wrap them, stick them on the back of my sleigh, and get my reindeer to carry me around so I can pop them down chimneys? Meet me halfway."

My brother moves off to the bar and, shortly after, returns with a lager for him, Guinness for me, and a bottle of water with a straw in it for Dad. Dad refuses to accept he is an alcoholic, so he asks for a bottle of water. This isn't the sole reason that he will not drink right now though. He physically shakes so bad that if he picks up, let's say, a full pint of lager, he would plaster the walls with it. So he has a bottle of water with a straw. This is just to start. He'll calm down slowly then maybe have half a lager with a straw then without the straw then a pint and then, when no one's around, crack open a bottle of whiskey and pass out.

During the evening I bring the three of us together, and we have some giggles, mostly at my dad's expense. He has a sense of humor and can take a joke. He feels proud around us and wants to show us off to the public as his boys.—Something which I am unreasonably not happy about. I don't see why he should feel proud about something he has had no input in. I can't seem to accept that he is happy with me and leave it at that; I seem to just feel the need to be angry about it. Dad tells us about some weird wheelchair-bound man he's befriended that he pushes around the market on a Saturday morning back near the flat where he lives and how the local football team he has a season ticket for are doing. He tells us how quiet it is in his block of flats, and he seems happy—frail and old but happy. It is strange to me. Apart from looking like death, he seems to be in good spirits. I drink a fair few pints, as does my brother. Dad gets through maybe two pints, maybe less, but definitely no more than two. We bring the night to a close. Dad and my brother walk off toward London Bridge and south of the river. I head off in the other direction along a still-busy Bishopsgate and along to Liverpool Street station.

I have twenty minutes or so until my train arrives. So I grab a coffee, sit down, read the paper, and its then that I burst into tears. I'm overwhelmed by the state I found my dad in and the shaking. I call my wife, but I can't get much out verbally down the phone to her. She just tells me that I should be looking forward to spending Christmas with my new young family and that my dad has put me through enough already. She tells me not to worry and that he knows if he wants help, we will be there for him. Trouble is, Dad doesn't recognize that he needs help. He fails to accept he drinks too much. Granted this night he's had two beers, but now left to his own devices, he'll polish off a bottle of scotch and then some when he gets home. Dad's secret drinking and denial of it absolutely amazed me. I had asked him, pleaded with him, begged, cried, and shouted at him for years to please stop drinking. "Please go to the doctor's and get help. I'll go with you. We can go together to wherever you want." But he just wouldn't help himself. Maybe the denial became the truth to him, I don't know. Is it possible that if you tell yourself enough times that everything is okay, you start to believe it? I looked into Alcoholics Anonymous, but it turns out that to give up the booze, you have to accept God. And there are two reasons that wouldn't work. One, there's no chance my dad would go for it, and two, if I had a choice of facing a pissed dad talking total bollocks or a religious one talking righteous bollocks, I'd take the drunk.

Maybe I failed him. Maybe I did; maybe I didn't. I'm not saying that I did do enough to have fixed him, and I'm not saying I just sat and watched him deteriorate. But when a policeman knocks at your door unexpectedly in the wet, cold darkness of the night holding his helmet in his hands, clutching it against his abdomen, and asks you, "Are you Martin Alberts, son of...?" When that snapshot moment happens to you in life, you'll forever and always ask yourself, *Did I do enough?*

PART 6

THREE MONTHS BACK, SUNNY MONTH OF MAY

My birthday's rolling in soon, and I'll be thirty-three, a good age. My wife always says "That's a good age" no matter what birthday it is. I judge myself against my age in certain ways, and I feel that thirty-three seems to be a fair enough reflection in my book. Looking at all that's happened in my life so far, I don't think I've under-or overachieved for my age. I'd say thirty-three and pretty much playing a par round. If I were to be twenty-three, and at this stage, I'd be five or six under. If I was eighty-three and in this predicament, I'd be well over par and crying in the clubhouse. But thirty-three it is, and people are rallying around me. I think they may suspect something is up; this worries me.

The lads have decided to take me on a "man outing" to Butlin's, of all places, for what I am told is an adult-only weekend. Not *adult* as in "pornographic," *adult* as in "no under eighteens allowed" at what is usually a family-filled holiday resort. I say resort, but Bognor Regis probably doesn't classify as a resort as such; it's more of a venue or a holiday camp or a shithole. Depends on how you look at it. But before all the crazy fun of a trip to Butlin's commences, my brother has decided we need to spend some time together also. He's got a big job on over at some massive posh London house and feels it'll do us both some good if we were to work together for a bit. I don't mind. I have no idea what I'm supposed to be doing with regard to building or decorating; but he'll give me a broom or a paintbrush, and we can work together, be together. Plus I can get out of my office for a few more days. It'll just be nice to see each other.

Since Dad left, things haven't changed much. In fact, nothing has changed. I found out that the world moves on and no fucker really cares, not much anyway. Obviously, people close to you try to care, but they have lives to be getting on with. And anyone on the cusp of your life or outside of it, well, they just crack on with it. Therefore, we—us, the hurt people—do just that as well; we just carry on too. I remember the day after Dad left, I was walking to the train station, and I noticed that the world hadn't changed. Sounds stupid saying it, but I was shocked by how nothing was any different. The sun was out; the small road running down the side of the train station was just as boring as it was the day before. People were cracking on with their day. The pubs were full, and people were joking around or working and just being all-round normal. All this normality just continued to be. I sat on a train on the way to London surrounded by normal. I sat there wearing sunglasses and looking out of the window up at the sky. I was thinking—or rather, hoping—that my dad's face would pop up out of one of the bright white puffy clouds. It didn't, so I sent him a shitload of text messages. Another thing that shocked me and took me by surprise that day was the fear that I'd never stop crying. I thought, *When will it actually stop? Surely it will stop. It must stop at some point.* In actual fact, from an hour or so after being told my dad was dead, I was sitting down and actually contemplating the time scale of grief.

Anyways, here I am outside this big London house to help my brother. We're not being closer just because of what's happened. We're close anyway. Also there's a slim chance that he can see that I'm crumbling on the inside and struggling daily. So it's either he's noticed or someone's gone and told him. I have my suspicions as to who may have penetrated the Bertie force field, but for now I'll just play it by ear. I've turned up with my best set of builder clothes that I can find. I want to blend in, and although I have no idea what I'm doing, I do like to try and look the part. So I've got a new pair of baggy brown shorts that are a hybrid of jeans material in a combat-trousers style, which I sat flicking paint on last night to make them look old. A brand-new tool belt—bloody nice one too, brown suede! On said tool belt is a hammer, spirit level, a selection of screws, nails, a screwdriver, and a cordless uncharged drill that I also flicked with paint last night. I probably won't need or, more to the point, be allowed to use any of this; but you never know.

When my brother turns up, he jumps out of the van looking smart. He's wearing smart dark jeans, a crisp white shirt, and shoes.

"What you doing?" I say to him angrily and confused.

"Whatdya mean? What the fuck are you doing?" he asks me back.

"Where's your builder's stuff?"

"What?" he says. "Why are you dressed like that?"

"Can we both stop asking questions at the same time? Why are you all smart when we're doing building and stuff?" I say.

"Well, seeing as we're going out later plus I need to go and meet the client first, I need to look representable. All my overalls are in the van. What are you wearing? And why do you have paint all over you? We haven't started yet? And you've not painted anything since nursery."

"Well, I wanted to look the part," I say.

"Have you gone out and bought a new tool belt?"

"Yeah, d'ya like it?"

"Whose tools are they?"

I look at the floor like a naughty schoolboy and mumble, "I bought them too. I've aged the stuff to look more professional."

"Come on, you idiot," he says whilst smiling at me. He puts his arm around me, and we both walk up the front steps to the front door of this house. It's a great, big, whiter-than-white town house in Fulham somewhere. Four floors including a basement, but I think the basement is a flat in itself. We wander up the twenty or so steps, and I'm warned not to say anything unless it a yes or no to a tea or coffee. I'm to be silent whilst my brother runs through all the final details with the owner. A very kind-looking, polite, and rather posh lady opens the door and immediately thanks us for being on time. She then apologizes for having to rush out very soon and tells us she only has a short amount of time to run through a few things. She then apologizes again that because of her busy schedule, she won't be able to make us any tea or coffee. *I'll be staying silent then,* I think to myself. My brother and the lady walk around going into room after room, which we'll be working on. They're both discussing instructions for each other and any last-minute ideas that spring to mind. My brother has a little notebook that he scribbles in furiously as the lady points out things to avoid, things that are urgent, and things that needn't be moved, touched, or tampered with.

This house is enormous. We're only doing three rooms, which are all downstairs; but there's possible scope for others to be worked on, and that's why they're both chatting away. I'm following the conversation loosely. It's not making much sense, but more importantly, I have other issues. A new and urgent problem has arisen. My major concern and all that I'm currently able to think about is that from out of nowhere, with zero warning, I really need a shit. Trouble is, I can't just run into the Jon whilst they're talking shop and unload; that's not polite in anyone's language. This Lamb Vindaloo I had last night from the Raj Pavillion is banging on the back door asking for an early release, and I'm not sure how long I can keep it bolted shut. Man alive, their discussion is taking an age. I thought she had to go. She said she was in a rush?

"Okay, so are we clear on everything?" the lady turns to me and my brother and says.

"Yep, it's all good. I'll give you my brother's number for today if you don't mind. Unfortunately, I've left my phone at home. But we'll be together all day, so I am contactable. And I have your number in my hand book, if needed," my brother tells her.

"There's something else," she says. "I can't quite think of what it is. There's definitely something else I was going to ask you to look at. Now what was it…" She stands there thinking, pondering what it is she's forgotten. *Get out the house* is all I can think. *Get out, out, out, hurry up.* But she just won't fucking leave! She's standing there looking all vacant, searching her mind over and over for the one thing she's forgotten. ITS NOT IN THERE I'm screaming to myself. *Just leave! Tell us tomorrow or never tell us at all, just go.* My bum is currently winking at me here. I start to think that the butt cheek firming exercises that my wife does daily are now not looking so stupid. I'm in trouble here. I need a movement and I need it fast.

"No, sorry," she says. "I can't remember. It's nothing of importance I'm sure. If I do happen to remember, I'll call you."

"Okay, that's not a problem. Well, we'll get started, and we'll see you this afternoon," my brother says.

"Great," she says. "Well, have a good day." I nod and grin, and my brother follows her outside. He's off to grab stuff from the van. And then, finally, she's gone. I burst into the nearest loo that I can find. Later I find out—would you believe?—there're five loos in this house. Who needs five? Anyway, it's not important. What is important is knowing that I can no longer hold on to this nasty piece of you-know-what and that it gets out of my system sharpish. I steam into the downstairs bathroom. It's a very nice and spacious room. It has been tiled floor to ceiling in white with the odd, random black tile. I bet it took ages to do and needed very specific placement to get the black tiles to look so random. It also has one sole white rug, one roll top standalone bathtub, one bidet, and one awesome-looking toilet of which I plant my arse upon.

My brother comes back into the house and finds that I'm nowhere to be seen.

"Bertie?" he shouts.

"I'm having a shit," I shout back through the door.

"Bloody hell, mate, we've only been here two minutes. I'll unload the rest of the van then, shall I? You just unload yourself," he shouts back. I bet he's pleased with his humor there. I can't see, but I bet he's chuckling away to himself and just a little bit proud. Then, my phone starts ringing. I don't recognize the number. But I do most definitely know who it is. It's the posh lady who owns the house, I bet it is. This room is tiled from the floor to the ceiling, and it echoes. My farts echoed when they left me. When I shouted to my brother, it echoed. And when I take this call, it will echo. I have to answer though. What if she comes back to tell us whatever it is she didn't tell us cos I didn't answer the phone? I answer the phone and cup the handset speaker part in both hands, bringing it as close to my mouth as I can, a bit like I'm holding a small baby to my face. I then try to attempt a nonechoing phone call.

"Hhhi," I sort of stutter and whisper down the phone. She hasn't heard me speak, so she doesn't know how I sound. I may well have a stuttered whispery voice for all she knows.

"Yes, it's me. I've just left you at my home where I had a memory lapse and had no idea what I needed you to look at. I couldn't remember until I got up the street, would you believe? Must be the fresh air," she says.

"Ooh oookay," I whisper in a husky nasty phone voice whilst trying not to rip one out of my arse on the echoing pan in the echoing room. Ever tried to stop a shit midflow? Don't is my advice.

"Are you all right?" the lady asks.

"Fiiiine, yep, all's fine here."

"Ah good. Well, anyway, the flush on the downstairs toilet is broken, so please can you take a look, and if need be, use one of the others? There's five in total, you know."

"Ooookayyy, that's fine, thanks," I manage to whisper and grunt back.

"Okay, cheerio."

"Bye."

Five! Fucking five. A five-to-one shot, and I hit the wrong one—unbelievable. Man alive, this is not good. I've only been a builder for less than a morning, and I've managed to leave an immovable object in the most posh of posh bathrooms. Crap, crap, crap. Well, I'm here now, so I decide to finish off, and then I'll think of what to do. So after the remanence of the Raj Pavillion has made its full escape, I think of what to do. Number 1 is open the window. First things first, get some air in. Then I think to myself, *Hold on, I've got my tool belt with me. Maybe I'll fix the toilet.* I quickly snap out of that bad idea. I'm not a builder, fixer, or anything like that. So instead I run and tell my brother. When he stops laughing, he tells me to get a bucket from the van, fill it up with water, and throw it down the toilet and to keep doing so until the poop has all gone. Then he tells me to go to the shops, get some toilet cleaner, come back, and deep clean the bathroom. By the time I've done all that, it'll probably be lunch, so I'll then have to go back out and get us lunch. I do all of the above.

I rather enjoy working over the next few days although I don't really do a lot apart from buy lunch, carry stuff around, and sweep up; but it's spending time out of my day-to-day shit with people I want to be with, and that helps me all round I think. During these days together, not once does my brother ask how I am feeling or anything awkward like that. He knows that I'm not running on all cylinders, and therefore, he is being supportive in other ways. He's a lot smarter than I give him credit for. Don't get me wrong, I still see him as the teenage idiot who once climbed out of the upstairs window, maneuvered himself across the ledge, and then climbed back in through the window on the other side just for a dare. But now I also see him as a type of therapist, and I did not expect that! I think I'll buy my wife a gift tonight. I think she may be the one who has penetrated the Bertie force field and then asked my brother for some help.

Next up, in what appears to be a secretly arranged rehabilitation program, is going to be the trip to Butlins! But before this hedonistic weekend of rampage ensues, I just need to get through two more days back at work. After that it'll be more time away from the real world and more time away from the dark-sided me. It's becoming apparent to me that if I'm with people who I get on with, keeping myself busy, and having fun, then I don't tend to sink into the dark clouds. Obviously, I like being around my family, but when I am, I feel pressured to do things all the time, things like odd jobs or tasks. This is what I tell myself anyway. It doesn't seem to make sense, what I am telling myself; and there are, of course, always exceptions to the rule. Some days I just want to sleep and ignore everyone. I want to avoid all interactions as this avoidance stops the thinking and ranting that goes on inside my mind. Sleep is sometimes the only cure. Some days I just want to sleep for a long time—some days maybe, or even a permanent time.

Back at work, and nothing whatsoever is happening. I arrived this morning at 8:00, which is an hour and a half later than normal, and I have basically finished what I will be doing today by 8:30 AM. Considering that I've been away for three days, that's pretty poor going on the work front. I call my wife just after 10:00 AM to see how she is and how everyone is. They're fine; no issues on the home front. After I put the phone down on her, at that very moment, I start to feel that I'm about to cry. I need to head out, so I head to the fire escape. After I arrive in the fire escape staircase, I begin the walk up the stairs and to the higher floors that are above mine. Floor 14 is cleared out. I assume this is due to the financial crisis and that plenty more space will free up over the coming months. I walk around the open floor crying. There's gray carpet, empty desks, and a few cables. This is all that's been left behind. It's silent and calm; it's ghostly. But inside me it is a very different atmosphere. Inside I'm screaming over and over again, *Need to do this, need to get that, I can fix this first, I should change this next, then I'll get onto this.* On and on and on it continues. It—whatever "it" is—just doesn't and will not fucking stop. Over and over the same issues are racing through my thoughts. I walk over to the window and stare down at what's below. Up until this moment, I had a huge fear of heights. I couldn't even stand looking at pictures that were up in the clouds; they would flip my stomach. Today, though, the height feels welcoming and warm. The numbness is now starting to sink in; this is surrounding me and makes the height of fourteen floors feel rather welcoming. This is new. This is a newbie. I'd not had this thought or feeling before. Well, not a practical realization of it anyway. Yeah, I'd thought how it would be to sleep forever, but now I seem to want to be in a place where I could actually make this happen. It's a strange feeling. The strangeness is that now there seems to be no feeling, no fear. I'm standing here crying. I don't know why. I'm standing on an empty floor contemplating horrific things, and yet I don't feel anything. I have no idea how long I've been here, and I don't care either. I know that I can't go back down to my floor, not until the tears have dried and my face isn't red and flush. I sit it out on the fourteenth floor and wait till I'm ready.

Nothing much happened for the rest of the day. I got back to my desk, signed a leaving card, had lunch, and left for the station at around 4:00 PM. I'd had enough of nothing for this day. This Wobble is still very much in full flow. I was hoping that it would piss off before I got home, but as it turns out, it gets worse the closer to home I get. Sitting in my car on the journey back from the station to my house, a song is playing by Stephen Fretwell, and I'm absolutely streaming with tears. It's not even a fucking sad song. It's about love and how this guy'll do whatever it takes to get the girl. It's romantic. I'm so fucking confused. I pull up outside my house and cradle my head in my hands, wiping the tears and trying to rub this shit feeling away. I put the entire day, everything that has happened, to just being tired. I'll have a shower, rest up, and I'll be fine. When I'm all set and not looking like a man who's been crying all day, I wander indoors with no evidence on show of what's going on in my head. I kiss my wife, ask how her day was, give the boys a cuddle, and take them upstairs for bath time. My wife's parents arrive at the house after about ten minutes of me being back. They're staying over for the night, so we order a takeaway and have a few drinks. Later in the evening, I tell them all that I'm tired. I want to shoot off to bed, it's about half-past nine. "Early start and all that," I say. And with that chat, I can escape the social interaction. I lie on my back and remain very still in bed, have a bit more of a cry, then I wait to nod off to sleep and escape this self-tortured hell for another day.

Friday evening arrives, and knowing that I'm off to Butlins in the morning with the lads makes me feel scared. I'm frantically worried that something will go wrong. I'm concerned that I'll wake up late or that my wife will need help with the kids whilst I am away. I worry that the shop on the corner will run out of milk so the kids can't have porridge. All sorts of crap. I think it'll be nice to make a nice meal for me and my wife for tonight. We can spend the evening chatting, having a drink and a nice meal, and generally relaxing. Enjoying our own company. Problem with this idea is that I'm involved in it. I'm falling to shit inside, and I'm unsure if I can keep this going much longer. Anyway, I need to get on. I'm making a curry. The rice is sitting there. It's almost cooked on the hob nearest to me, the front left one. I have, in fact, made two curries: one is spicy and one is mild. They're both bubbling away on the back hobs. I've slowly cooked them so that they absorb as much spice and flavor as possible. I hate that word—*flavor*. I hate the part in cooking shows where they all eat and tell us how wonderful it tastes too. And the obligatory "Ooooh, that smells soooo good." *Just eat the fucking food,* I always think or say out loud. Nonetheless, dinner is cooking away nicely. Along with the curries I've made a lemon chutney and a carrot salad. The chapatis are in the oven, and there's a stack of cold beer in the fridge.

There's one other small issue though. Since I woke up this morning, I have been afraid of my own wife and kids. I can't be near them, and as a result, I have been hiding in the kitchen making all this food and using the dinner as an excuse to avoid them. The food looks nice. I can't do much more cooking apart from waiting, and then I'll bring it all together at the end and serve it up. Just waiting on the rice and watching that nothing burns.

I need to cry.

I stir both curries, turn the back hobs off, and put the lids on to keep them juicy and warm.

I'm struggling to breathe.

I switch the oven off; the chapatis will keep warm in there, and they'll not cook anymore or burn.

I'm containing my hyperventilation inside.

Dinner is now all ready to go to the table at any point.

I can't swallow; my throat feels as if it's closing.

I left Poppadom's on the table, and my wife has tucked into them. I realize that there's none left. But I have made a chutney especially for them. I am ranting at myself.

"You've eaten all the 'Doms," I say.

"Yes, sorry, Bertie, I have. I can pop out and get some more. I hadn't realized that that was all we had."

"I made lemon chutney for them, could you not have waited?" I snap.

"Does it really matter?"

"Forget it, doesn't matter," I say. But not in a nice "forget it" way. Instead I say it in a moody, nasty, snappy way. Thing is, it does fucking matter; it really matters. It wasn't supposed to go like this. We should have done it another way—don't know which way for sure but not like this. I start to get angry, so I down a beer. Then I notice the nearest hob to my left isn't switched on; the rice isn't cooking. SHIT. This is fucking shit. Now I'm really angry.

"Aaaah, for fuck sake," I scream.

My wife stares at me in shock. "Calm down, Bertie. It's only Poppadoms."

"It's not just fucking Poppadoms," I say. I look around at what I need to do: cook the rice through, serve the curry, get the carrot salad out of the fridge, and leave the chutney in the fridge. Take the chapatis out of the oven, put things in serving dishes, cook the rice—I still need to cook the rice. I can't do it; I can't do it. It's too much. I grab a wooden chopping board and smash it in half across the edge of the kitchen worktop. I then do this again with one of the halves, so I now have three pieces of chopping board. There's one piece left in my hands and two on the floor. I stand back, take note of the situation, down another beer, and calmly pick up the broken pieces, which I put in the bin. My wife says nothing. She must now be annoyed with me because of the reaction to the Poppadom fiasco. I start to try to tell myself it's okay, that I can do this, I can put the heat on for the rice, everything is okay, I can do this, I can win this battle. I put the hob on and stare at it. Problem is, I can't do this. I can't cope; I can't cope with cooking fucking rice.

I quickly turn everything off, and then I walk out of the house. Shaking, crying, and screaming in silence, I walk off at a quick pace towards nowhere. I don't know where I'm going, but I know what I need. I just need a place to sit, a park bench or something—just as long as I am away from everyone. I just need to be alone, and I don't need to see a single soul. At the same time, I have no idea who it is that I'm trying to run away from. The shaking and the need to scream is raging through me; my mouth is open and my jaw is taut. The tears are now in full flow, and I silently scream to the heavens. I wander around, looking for somewhere to go; but I realize that there is nowhere. How do you run away from yourself? How can you disappear from your own self? Because that's what I want to do; that's what I need to do. I need not to be Bertie anymore; I can't be Bertie anymore. Whilst walking around, I am unable to find anywhere that's suitable, so I just stop walking. I stop down the middle of a small footpath that has walls running down either side and nothing else. I stop and stand there looking at the wall. It's just a wall; it's about eight-feet high, red brick, nothing special or exciting about it. Importantly though, there's nothing on the other side of it or facing opposite to it other than a mirror image of itself. It's here that I choose to stop and hope to God that no one comes along.

Standing still, out in the night air, and staring at a fucking wall, is this it? Is this what I have become, running away from rice and an evening with a beautiful woman with whom every inch of my living and working soul I adore? Have I now become an oddball, a street merchant in a hoodie? Fuck, I have. All I can think is *Fuck, fuck, fuck.* Anger, fear, tears—everything starts to fade away, and into a dullness I'll drift. I look away from the wall and stare off toward the end of the footpath where the street runs across. I look at that for a while. It takes me quite some time to pluck up the energy to move, and when I do, I head for home. I get back indoors and say nothing, nothing as to why I smashed up the chopping board, nothing about running out, nothing. Let's just pretend nothing has happened, and let's not say a word. We watch a bit of TV sitting in separate rooms, and then after an hour or so, I feel it's late enough. I go to bed.

In the morning I grab my bag, kiss my wife, and head off to meet the lads. We don't speak of anything that happened last night; there's no need to. I feel much better today. I have had a release of all the shit, and now I'm good, fixed, back in the game. I probably just needed a little outburst. All that is now on the agenda is fun. Me, Bigface, Deckchair, Smudger, Ron Daly, Helpful and my Brother, all meet up outside the London Bridge train station by the cash machines that are opposite to the bus stops at 12:00 PM sharp. When it comes to our jollies, its been a "12:00 London Bridge meet" for quite some time now, regardless of where we are going. Not sure how that started; it has just been this location point for the start of play.

Smudger, the good lad, already has the beer for the train. Bigface is at the bar in the Oast House pub, which is situated just inside the station, and he has a prearranged whip, meaning that he'll bill us later for all beer consumed. Helpful has everyone's tickets, train times, and platform information; and I'm wearing a nice hat. So we're pretty much all set. It's going to take us just under two hours on the train, so Smudger has bought three cases of inoffensive lager to keep us going. But we need to be smart here. You don't drink your own beer until the train's bar has been emptied. The last thing you want is to run out of your own beer, hit the bar on the train, and then find out that the few seasonal drinkers have beat you to it and drained it. Always remember to never drink your own resources first; it's vital. We learned that lesson the hard way whilst on a trip to Paris a couple of years back.

There's still about twenty-five minutes before we leave, so we all join Bigface in the Oast House. Man alive, this pub is grim. The carpet is a mix of brown, red, yellow ish sticky, bald in places and patches with added dobs of black rubber splodge. I don't know what these splodges are, but do I know that if you were to tread on one, you'd probably remain there. The whole place is dark inside, which is odd in itself as the pub isn't underground and it does have windows. The only light is from the fruit machines and the fading bulbs behind the bar. Everything in it this pub is so minging and dirty that it actually makes the place really dark. But hey ho, Bigface seems happy enough.

"Weheey! Lads! Right, fifty quid, please," Bigface announces excitedly. He does this and claps once, keeping his hands together and then rubs them whilst tucking his elbows into his sides. He does this with an added stupid little dance. This fifty quid will be our beer fund for the next two days. Well, it won't actually last two days, but it's a start; and we all believe in the innocent thought that we won't get through 350 quid solely on beer.

"I ain't putting in fifty," Smudger says. "I bought this lot," and he points to the three cases.

"Shut up and don't be tight. Give Bigface your money. I arranged the train tickets, but I'm not banging on about that, am I?" says Helpful.

"Fair point. Here you go," Smudger says and hands over the money just like that. Smudger is easily persuaded to part with cash when there's a whip involved and when someone might insinuate that he's tight. Bigface takes all our cash. He really is a great whip holder; he's got a massive friendly face, and as he is also a smidge under seven feet tall, he gets served at the bar the quickest. We have a quick couple of beers in this delightful establishment, and then Helpful tells us that it's time to move out and to head to Platform 13—unlucky for some. Unlucky for the people who get our carriage!

We all jump on the train at our designated carriage and go to our seats. All of us chuck our bags in the overhead rails and then head for the buffet cart. On these journeys, although we have seats, we never use them; we go to the bar and spend the journey there. Five minutes or so after boarding, the train has pulled away and BigFace has got a round of drinks in for us all to enjoy. We're standing in the train buffet area chatting away when, from nowhere, Deckchair bursts through the connecting doors. His face is borderline purple, and he's blowing out of his arse for breath and struggling to stand up. He's got sweat pouring all over his bald head.

"What the fuck has happened to you?" I say.

"Well, I got on the train with you lot," he says, panting out of his arse, "walked to our seats, saw you lot putting your bags up, and then thought, *Shit, I've left my bag in that shitty pub.* So I jumped off and ran back to get it. I'm not spending all weekend in the same outfit. Problem was, Helpful's got the tickets."

"I do have the tickets," Helpful says.

"So I had to race up the platform navigating through a crowd of people, through the security gate, and grab my bag from the bar. I get to the bar. There's no one in there, just my bag, so I grab it and turn back to head for the train." His breathing is steadying, and his face is less crimson. He continues, "The wanker on the ticket gate wouldn't let me back through though. I tried to tell him that I just forgot my bag, my friend has my ticket who's on the train, but he wouldn't have it. So I jumped the barriers."

"You? You jumped the barriers?" says Smudger in a confused and slightly sarcastic voice. Deckchair isn't the most agile of beings.

"I did, then I ran like a madman for the train. Up the slope, dodged all the people on the platform again and another guard, plus I've got the fucker from the gate who's now fucking chasing me, and I just made it. The doors were bleeping as I dived on and hit the carriage floor. I actually dived onto the floor of the carriage. The guard was almost there at the door as we pulled out."

"I can't believe you found someone slower than you," says Smudger.

"He would have caught you, you fat shit! Give me beer. God, I'm fucked," Deckchair announces. Helpful then comes back into the bar after a brief disappearing act.

"Where you been?" I say.

"Enjoy your shit?" says Smudger with a huge smile on his face.

"No, actually, Smudge. Well, I thought, seeing as none of us have been to Bognor Regis before, that I'd have a quick look on my laptop to see what we can do whilst we're down there," Helpful says.

"You brought your laptop?" I say.

"Yes, the train does have Wi-Fi."

"So what sort of cultural and fascinating opportunities await us?" I ask.

"I don't know. I had to leave the carriage. I had an argument," he says.

"With who?" Helpful doesn't argue with anyone.

"I was sat amongst four of the most irritating people money could buy. Three blokes and some annoying woman. They're sitting there, sharing a bag of crisps."

"And that annoyed you?" said Deckchair.

"In part, yes. Along with the fact they're all wearing Bluetooth headsets, and along with the fact they will not shut up about these poxy crisps they're eating."

"What?" I say.

Helpful continues, "One of them's holding a bag. He goes, 'Mmmm, these are really nice. Try these.' The next one goes 'Ooh they're nice, well nice.' He then says, 'You've gotta try these. These are proper nice,' in a new accent that he didn't have seconds ago. 'Have you seen these before? Not seen these before. They're really good.' Another one pips in with 'I've not seen them either. Watch out I'm going in for another,' and he nudges me whilst 'going in for another' and adds some aeroplane noise. This goes on and on—'Mmmm top crisps, top crisps, well nice, yeah tops these.' The straw snapped for me when one goes 'Pukka crispee a reeenis these are.'

"I couldn't take it anymore, so I lost it and said, 'LOOK! There's four of you, one bag of crisps, you've been banging on about them for what? Five minutes? EAT THE FUCKING THINGS. SHUT UP. THEY STINK. Fucking sitting there with your Bluetooth headset on."

"Whoooa, steady," Smudger says.

"I know," says Helpful. "I felt instantly bad, put the laptop away, and came back here. I plan to hide here now, with you lot, all the way to Bognor."

An hour or so later, we arrive at Bognor Regis station. Funny—well, I think it's funny—that when I was little and I first heard of Bognor Regis, I thought it must be abroad as it sounded too tropical. We all jump in taxis from outside the station that take us to the resort, but upon approach, all is not as it should appear I think to myself, *There's a lot of kids running around for a start, not what I would expect for an adult-only weekend.* We get dropped off and walk across the car park, down a gravel track, and look for the reception. However, as we approach the reception, we can hear a loud speaker that announces, "Go-carting competition starting at four. Arts and craft center is now closed." Go-carting, arts and crafts…sounds a bit suspect. Then we see a crocodile walking around; well, a bloke in a fluffy crocodile suit. I'm not sure this is right.

"This ain't right. This is an adult-only weekend," Smudger says.

Bigface tell us not to worry and that they're probably getting shot of the kids and families after six or something like that. We get to the reception desk and start sorting out our rooms whilst ignoring all the facts, ignoring them right up until my brother asks the receptionist. "Is this the adult-only weekend?"

"No," the receptionist says, "it's the Elkie Brooks weekend."

PART 7

NOW

Later, after the attention and the weekend away, I find out that my wife's parents had seen me in my car back on the night that they had stayed over. They saw me clutching my face with my head cradled in my hands... This is bad. This means that this issue could well be or is probably now out in the public domain. This also means that people will be different around me. However, I am not accepting anything. This issue will pass. I know this. Just tired, that's it. Onwards and upwards!

Saw an odd thing this morning—a fight on the Tube! Not that a fight on the London Underground is odd in itself, but the actual fight, the physicality of this one, was. A guy was sitting quite happily on the Tube with his headphones, playing music loud enough so that all the carriage could hear. This does irritate most people, not me though! This is one of the very few things, in fact, that I find the least irritating as I always like to try to guess the song that's being played. This guy's headphones were tuned in to either a mishmash of a famous hits album or just on a "popular music" shuffle. It was belting out all sorts, and I managed to name three from the first four correctly, right until we got to Moorgate. The reason that I only managed to get up to the three correctly named songs got on at Barbican. At Barbican, en route to Moorgate, this guy gets on and sits next to the "Music Man." The new guy to the carriage was clearly annoyed by the sounds. He sat, huffed, looked at me, shook his head, and raised his eyes to the top of his head. I think he wanted my approval or acknowledgment. I wanted him to stop distracting me as I was not sure if it was U2…no, hang on, it was Simple Minds. Now I was torn between "Don't You Forget About Me" or "Alive 'n' Kicking." I waited a little longer whilst trying to tune my hearing into the Music Man. You have to get the song before the chorus starts, those are my rules. As I was attempting to zone in, "New Guy" was getting increasingly flustered with the noise, but instead of tapping the guy on the shoulder and asking if he wouldn't mind turning it down, he leaned in toward him then he pulled Music Man's right headphone away from his head and then he said, "Turn it down."

Music Man took immediate offense to this. "What the fuck are you doing?"

"Turn it down or off," said Flustered.

"Get your fucking hands off me." Music Man was looking really shocked. I don't think he liked having his ears touched by a stranger on the London Underground.

"Look, mate, just turn it down," said Flustered.

"Fuck you," Music Man said and then sat back and replaced his headphones. Flustered then went for them again! Music Man ducked to his left but, due to the close proximity, couldn't avoid the swipe from Flustered. His headphones were half on, half off. Both then started to throw weak punches and slaps, but because they were so close sitting side by side and the tube was busy, there was zero room to maneuver. They couldn't swing, couldn't get enough leverage into a decent punch. It was brilliant and educational to watch. If you're not Bruce Lee and don't have a one-inch punch, then seated Tube fighting is not for you. The fight was halted as we arrived at Moorgate because Music Man had to get off. He still gave Flustered the finger and mouthed "Fuck you" as the train pulled away running alongside him as he walked up the platform, which I thought was a nice touch.

This morning, pre-Tube fight, I had been to the other side of the city for a conference. Well, it was more of a sales pitch from a group of firms who had promised to do all our work for us at a fraction of the cost. All we had to do was get everyone in London to train up a new set of staff then relocate our efforts to somewhere in Asia and fire everyone based in the UK. Well, not all but most of them. Sounds harsh? Get used to it. It's the new working model, and it's not going to change for a long time. I'm not interested in this model, not yet however.

After arriving back at the office and doing some admin, I set up the meeting to make the shareholders and senior management aware of the proposals and what risks it will bring to the firm in its current state—the main risk being I don't want to move to India or China. Later that day I'll tell them that we have subject matter experts here in the UK, that we are in a current climate right now where stability is vital, and that change of such a drastic proportion could be very costly. And if it comes down to it, I will let them know that I cannot support such a move and would happily accept a golden handshake if they feel the need to progress in such a manner.

The meetings are now firmly in the diary for the end of this quarter as this is when the key rich people are due to arrive for a booze-filled dinner paid for by the firm. Now, that's me done for the day work-wise, so I pop outside from my glass-room office to see how things are "on the ground." The team isn't the worst bunch of people; they seem happy. They know no different, and they don't want different either. They're old—not physically old, just old think-ers. Change, drive, and ambition is something that they walk past on the way to work, not something that they would bring in with them. They don't know about the Asia proposal, and it's best not to tell them either. I'm actually on their side, not that they know or care.

Coming up soon is the birthday of a wife of one of the team members. Within this team they all know all the family of the oth-ers—they know their names, jobs, hobbies, pretty much everything. The husband who works here has brought in a card and is sending it round for signing. I'm not going to sign this. I don't know the woman and I don't want to. I don't go to the functions that the team has either. Last year they had a Christmas do on a Saturday? Who, whilst working in the City, wants to come back here on a Saturday, with your family, to spend more time with the people you already spend all day with? This guy, whose wife's birthday it is, has bought her an original Stevie Wonder vinyl album—to go with a new record player, I assume. He has the record with him and is reading the songs aloud to the group.

"Oh, didn't know he did 'Light My Fire,' 'Yester-Me, Yester-You, Yesterday,'" he says.

"Yep I think she'll like this 'My Cherry Armour,'" he announces.

"It's pronounced 'My Sherri A-More.'" He's quickly corrected by a woman on the team. This woman has taken mass delight that instead of "Cherie" the guy said "Cherry." This woman is a bitch. She makes sure that the rest of the floor hears all about "Cherrygate" for the rest of the day. Like I say, a bitch. Mental note, she's first out the door if we go to Asia.

I've had to start drinking in another pub at lunchtimes now due to my change in work location; but the City is a square mile, so there's always a friend close by. Plus the new pub, the Kensington, has friendlier staff, cheaper beer, and no holes in the ceiling. I meet with Smudger for what is known as Thirsty Thurdays.

"August Bank Holiday coming up. What's the plans, Smudge?" I ask as I hand over a Stella in the new style glass. They look like large wine glasses, and Smudger has taken massive offense to them; so I always get his drink in one.

"Why do you have to do that, you Wanker?" he says, looking at the glass.

"Because I am a Wanker. I wouldn't do it if I wasn't," I tell him.

"Going to me mum's on Sunday as per usual, and on Monday, there's a few of us going to the club. There's a BBQ and some other shit going on to raise money for the club itself." He's talking about the football club we both once played for, but after an incident, I stopped playing.

"Nice, sounds like a good day."

"Come along. Be good to see Bertie and family back at the club."

"Can't, mate. It's probably for the best if I never go back. Plus the in-laws are having a thirtieth wedding anniversary bash on Saturday out in the sticks, so there'll be family around all bank holiday weekend. There's plans for Friday through to Monday. I don't know what they are yet. I just know that the kids are going to my aunts, I have to get a train tomorrow afternoon after work to somewhere or other, and that I'm getting picked up at the station."

"Well, if you change your mind or plans, we'll be there from about 12:30."

We finish up our lunch beers, and I grab a KFC on the way back to the office. On my way back, I have to walk passed the Tower of London where there's plenty of people after your money. Charities, homeless people, and of course, the old-fashioned pickpockets. I see a young girl there sitting down with a sign. I don't read it, but as I feel a bit fat and I'm already full up on Guinness, I give her the KFC that I have just bought. I threw the drink that came with the meal in the bin after leaving the takeaway because I didn't want to carry it, so as I hand it to her, I apologize for not having anything to wash it down with. She takes the news well and seems happy to have a large Zinger meal. This exact gesture was once a common occurrence that I continued with for some time. If I saw a homeless person as I entered a supermarket or a fast food place, I would grab something for them whilst in there. As I say, I did this for some time right up until one day when I saw one of the fuckers taking the food back into the shop and asking for a refund! At that moment I thought to myself that that was it, there it was. There was my nice bit and now that's fucked and I'm back to being an arsehole again. Still, just for today, I'll step back to that nice person for a second.

Friday comes round, and I've finished up at the office early and headed off to the station. I'm getting the train out to Suffolk where I'll be picked up at the local station by my father-in-law. After getting picked up in the arsehole end of nowhere, we're going to the venue that will host Saturday's party to have a family dinner; the venue being their enormous garden.

"I need a ticket to Diss," I tell the ticket office woman with a smile on my face as I admire the private joke.

"Standard. First. Single. Return?" she calls out at me. These people don't speak like we do; they seem to just bleep in a controlled manner at the same constant tone.

"Just a single. What's the difference in price for first class compared with standard?"

"Standard is 63.40. First is 87.20" gets bleeped back at me.

"Strange amounts," I say but there's no response. "Just the standard single fair, please."

"Insert your card." Another bleep. "Here's your ticket."

"Thanks very much. What platform is the train leaving from?"

"There's no trains," she then tells me.

"What? You've just sold me a ticket, and there's no trains?"

"It's bank holiday weekend." She tells me this as if it's now all clear and that I'll understand. I clearly do not.

"Right?" I say, confused.

"Maintenance on the track."

"Is this a fucking windup? You've just sold me a ticket, and at no point did you think about telling me that there's no trains?"

"There are buses leaving from outside the station," she bleeps back.

I'm fucking livid now. "And it's the same price as the trains? Hang on, does it even have first class?"

"You didn't want first class."

"You tried to sell it to me."

"Outside the station where the buses are leaving is a staff member who can help you further. Please move along, sir. You're holding up the queue."

"Well, fuck me sideways," I say to her. I walk off, furtherly confused and pissed off. Another wonderfully enjoyable moment in my life spent interacting with the great people of the United Kingdom's public transport services.

I get on the bus and phone my wife to tell her that I'll be an additional hour and 20 minutes because I'm on the bus and not the train. This is my fault apparently as I should have checked and as "Dad doesn't want to wait that long." I will get a taxi so he can have a glass of wine. It's pretty enjoyable on the bus. In fact, it was a nice change. It took some time to get out of Central London, but after that the journey wasn't too bad at all. Before I bought my nonexistent train ticket, I had secured some provisions for the trip: a six-pack of lager, pork scratchings, and a tub of rollmops. Seeing as I was not planning on speaking to anyone, I didn't care much about the smell I was going to create. I have a book and a game on my phone and am, in fact, very happy.

That night, when I got to Diss, I called from the station booked and took a taxi straight to the venue for dinner. The wife's family were all there; it was a pretty normal affair: wine, chitchat, food. We sat in an open planned conservatory backing onto a marquee in the garden. Tomorrow night this would all be filled with people from all over the place who have come to celebrate a marriage that's lasted. These people are nice people; they're all getting along, they speak to one another politely, and they behave themselves. I can't imagine any of these people telling a train ticket seller to "Fuck me sideways." Talk then moves onto tomorrow night, and I've been asked to help behind the bar, which is brilliant news. I love working behind a bar, did it as a teenager whilst at college. If only it paid more than 3.50 an hour, I'd still be doing the job today.

The beers I had on the bus along with the wine at dinner and the rollmops mean that the next morning, I happen to not be in a particularly good way. I do feel a bit rough, but I'll have some toast and I'll be okay. We had stayed that night at my wife's aunt's house about five miles away from the party. We'd left the car at the venue as my wife and I were drinking, so I now need to go and get the car back this morning. The day is now a fully packed event: haircuts, new suits, dresses, and meeting up with long-lost family members. My wife's dad just turned up outside to get me. He's taking me back to his place so I can get the car, and then after we do that, we're going over to another family house where all the girls are meeting for a breakfast and fingernail painting session. I don't know why I have to attend that bit.

We're on the way over to get the car, and I'm lost directionally; there's only green bushes and fields to my left and right. I don't see anything distinguishing at all. My father-in-law tells me that the area is used for farming grass. Real garden-lawn grass. Who'd have known or thought that you actually farm that? We get to the house, and I have to help out a bit. I ferry around a few chairs and tables, run up and down the garden, then I help to set up the bar. It's nothing too strenuous; but my body is oozing out the booze from last night, and I am sweating buckets. That piece of toast I had to fix this hangover wasn't enough. I'm running on empty here. I don't feel great, but I'm hardly going to fess up that I'm hungover to the in-laws. Usually my wife announces it for me. "Martin's hungover," she'll say within a minute or two of us entering a family soiree. It is usually the truth after all. For now, I'll just sweat this one out. We, the father-in-law and I, finish our errands; and he tells me to get my car and to follow him back to where my wife is so that I know where the fuck I actually am and I can then take her over to the other house where the girls are all getting their shit together. He doesn't put it quite like that, but that's what's what.

As we drive down these country lanes, my guts are churning. I feel sick. I'm going to throw up, and I need to stop. I'm sweating like a madman in a sauna, and I have got to stop the car. The problem is, I can't pull over. There's nowhere to actually pull over, and if I did pull over, I can hardly blow chunks in front of my father-in-law on the morning of his special day. I devise a plan to lose him. He's in front of me; so I'll slow up and get caught at the lights, or I can take a wrong turn. Problem is, there's not a fucking traffic light in sight— nothing at all for love or money. The roads are winding and bending, but there's no alternative route on offer, not even a farm track. Every fucking time I slow up, so does he. He's clearly concerned I'll get lost. For fuck's sake, I wish he would just stop giving a shit and speed off! I open a window with my options now firmly planted on Plan B; Plan

A is clearly not working. Plan B is to breathe some fresh air, and if needed, I will vom out the window whilst driving. I quickly realize that you can't drive a coupe and lean out of the window to chuck. It's because you're seated too low down and too far away from being able to actually extend your neck far enough to get the sick out of the car and onto the great British countryside. However, luckily, just by having the window open, the wave of nausea seems to pass, which is good news. The fresh air is working. Plan B, you beauty!

Then *boom*—from nowhere I vomit directly over the steering wheel, which is at such a force that it hits the center of the wheel and leaps back at me like a laser and splashes all over my shirt. I sit in shock for a second, still driving and not knowing what to do. *Boom*—I chuck again. Same result. The steering wheel is solid across the middle where you bang it to beep the horn, and this is creating a reflector for my puke. *Boom*—a third time. This time I was looking down at myself, and the projectile hits me on my lap and in between my legs. I'm now in a state of shock and bewilderment. What the fuck am I going to do now? I'm still driving behind my father-in-law on the way to pick up my wife. Oh dear, oh dear, there's a shed load of it everywhere. Between my legs is a small swimming pool of vomit. It absolutely stinks, and I'm wet through from my own puke that's running from my chest to my knees. There's a roundabout! You beauty, father-in-law goes straight, I go left and hammer it off up the road to lose him. After about a mile or so I stop. The puke has been absorbed, mostly by the seat, and the puke pool is now a small-sized puddle. Now I have to call my wife.

"Hi, where are you, Bertie? Dad's just got back," she asks.

"Not sure."

"Can you find your way back here?"

"Errrr, yeah, I can. But can your dad not drop you off to the nail thing?"

"Well, yes, probably. Why?" Oh good god, I can feel the disappointment coming down the line. "Why, Bertie, what's happened? Have you had an accident?"

"Yes, yes I have," I say.

"Oh my god, are you okay?"

"I'm fine, don't worry."

"The car? Is the car okay?" she says.

"It's okay-ish, needs a wash."

"Martin, what's happened?"

I turn into a twelve-year-old; and I slowly, shyly, and shamefully announce, "Babe, I've been sick."

"Where?"

"All over myself…whilst driving."

Silence. She says nothing for a bit. I think she's absorbing what has just been said. Most wives at this stage would probably say something like "You're joking right?" but my wife knows better.

"Martin, just come back to the house."

"No chance," I reply.

"Just come back, and we can get you cleaned up."

"With all your family there? No thanks. I'll find a shop and get some clothes or something. I'll fix this. Get your dad to take you over to the girls, please, and I'll get myself and the car back to where it should be in time for you to go and pick up Nana."

"Bertie, it's fine."

"Bye, speak later," I say quickly and hang up.

Well, Plan A and B were a shower of shit, so Plan C it is! Onwards and upwards! I drive off in the same direction I was heading before I stopped. I'm on the lookout for anything that will help the situation. I pass a sign for a country manor-type hotel, looks very nice. What have I got to lose? I pull into the next turn, go up the drive, and park up on the gravel. It's always gravel at these big places, isn't it? Standing at the reception, I look a bit damp, nothing too obvious, but there is a certain smell about me. There're no guests about, which is good, and the receptionist appears with a smile. He's a young lad and looks like he's going be happy to help me; he seems keen and eager.

"Good morning, welcome to Holton Lodge. How can I help you?" he says.

"I'd like a room, please."

"For the night?" he says.

"No, not actually for that long," I say.

"Sorry, sir. We don't sell them by the hour."

"Look, mate, I'm in a tight spot. I'm covered in my own chunder. I need a shower, some clothes, and a car cleaning kit if possible. I need to get back to my in-laws at some point who are having a thirtieth wedding anniversary party tonight, and I'm not even sure where it is exactly."

"That is a tight spot," he says.

"I'll give you fifty quid cash if you can help me."

"Room 105 is free for now," he says with a smile. I like this kid. He's normal and helpful. "I'll see what clothes I can find for you, sir. Here's the key. If you can just leave the room as you find it, I would be very appreciative."

"Great," I say. "You won't know that I was there. Thanks very much indeed."

I clean myself up, throw my clothes in the bin; and then as promised, the young receptionist arrives with some new ones. What a nice lad.

"I have managed to get some trousers from the porters' staff room and a shirt from the waiters' changing area."

"Amazing, thanks so, so much."

"No luck with the car cleaning equipment I'm afraid."

"Never mind, beggars and all that," I say.

"Sir, please don't leave your old clothes in that bin."

"Sure."

I give the guy fifty quid as promised and head back to the car. I also manage to borrow a towel so I don't have to sit in my own sick. Plan C is going pretty well so far, albeit I'm dressed as a waiter and the car absolutely stinks. I drive to the nearest town and get a bundle of cleaning stuff for the car—carpet shampoo, air fresheners, scrubbers, and scrapers—and then I head back in the direction of where we are staying. As my wife is now out and I am no longer covered in sick, I can get back over there and get to work on the car. So that's what I do. I get a little lost, but I eventually make it there in the end. I start about cleaning the car. I scrub that mother to within an inch of its life for a good couple of hours whilst leaving all the doors and windows open. And, it's worked, the smell has gone and the cars come up a real treat, Plan C is killing it today! Now it's just a case of getting a haircut. I'll do that in the village we're staying in, and I think that I'll also have beer to celebrate. I'm on a real high at the moment. I haven't felt sad or bad about anything for days now; I knew it would pass. It's all gone, no more clouds. Brilliant, it must have been just a stressful time. Now I'm through it, and I'm out the other end, quite a relief actually.

Haircut done, I wander into the nearest pub and wait at the bar. When the barman arrives, he immediately tells me that he doesn't need me till seven. I have a confused look on my face for a moment then I realize, he thinks I'm a waiter. Must be the lapels.

"Okay," I say. "Can I have Guinness till then though, please?" I don't feel the need to correct him. As long as he doesn't want me to start clearing tables, what do I care what people think I do for a living? It's a bright sunny day. I've got the entire afternoon now free, and I plan to spend it alone doing as little as humanly possible.

A few hours have passed. The family and friends all start to roll into the village and a good few are milling about back at the aunt's house where I am staying. I head back to the house from the pub. I know a few of the people, and I end up chatting to a nice couple who have come up from the West Country. Then my wife arrives from the nail and girly day thing. She looks amazing—all dressed for the party, hair and nails done. She looks great. I love it; I love that I fancy my wife.

"Feeling better?" she says, looking at me, eyebrows raised, slightly cynical.

"Much better. Thanks, darling. You look amazing."

"Bertie was sick on himself today," she tells the couple I'm speaking to.

Fuck me, she's not been back ten seconds and she's announced it. I assume that the mother-and father-in-law also know. Ah well, we all make mistakes. The West Country folk seem concerned for my welfare. They actually look concerned. They say things like "Oh dear, that sounds nasty. Hope you are better now."

"He was hungover," my wife says.

Bingo, there you are—the "Bertie is hungover" statement.

"It could've been something else," I say.

"Whilst driving," she then adds.

We then peel away from the group, or rather, they peel away from us.

"Is the car clean?" I am asked.

"Yes," I confidently respond with a stern nod.

"Good because I have to drive over to pick up Nana in an hour. How are you getting over to the party?"

"Don't know. Can't I get a lift with one of this lot?"

"Where did you get that shirt from? I know that Dad wants help behind the bar, but aren't you're taking it a bit too seriously?"

"No," I remonstrate back. "I borrowed these clothes. They're not mine. I'll get changed in a bit." I had actually grown into this outfit and had started to quite like it. And if I hadn't been called out on it by my wife, I probably would have worn it to the party.

"From who?" she says. "Oh look, never mind, Bertie. Just hurry up and get changed now. I'll drop you at the party, and then I'll go over and pick up Nana."

"Right." I nod in her direction then pop upstairs, shower (again), get changed (again), and come back down where she is waiting for me.

We walk out of the house and over to the car. My wife is first to the door as I had parked driver's side to curb.

"Oh my good god. Martin, it stinks," she says.

I open my door, and sadly, she's right. I must have gone nose blind whilst cleaning it. How did this happen? The warm weather, I'm thinking. Leaving the car in the sun after the clean and having all windows and doors shut must have rallied the aroma; it's pretty potent.

"I'm going to gag," she says, clutching her mouth.

"That is odd. I cleaned it." I'm a tad confused.

"Well, you clearly haven't. The air freshener that you've added is just making it worse, Martin. Alpine air freshness and the contents of your stomach. What a lovely way to smell on the night of my mother and father's thirtieth wedding anniversary." I don't have much to say; there's not a lot to say. "Get in the car, Bertie," I am ordered.

We've been driving for about five minutes, and I start to get used to the smell. That's what must have happened; I was so close to it for so long I became immune to it.

"It's not that bad when the windows are down and we get the breeze coming through," I say.

"Don't" is her firm and sole response.

The party was a really good night after the initial malarkey of the day. And when my wife finally had time to relax, she really enjoyed herself too. The only issue she had was that Nana insisted on having the windows closed whilst in the car because she didn't want to feel the chill.

PART 8

DOCTORS

Thinking that all was well and that the clouds were now gone forever was a stupid thing to think. After we got back from the weekend away and picked up the kids from my aunt's house, I fell into a silent trap that lasted an entire week. At home I would avoid my wife as best as possible. I would cook all day long or do the gardening. When returning home from work, I would hope that a film was on that she wanted to watch. I would hope that the film would be something I wouldn't want to watch just so that I could make the excuse and head to bed. I would lock myself away in the bathroom and cry when the clouds were at their fiercest. I do find some comfort in the silence that sits around me and can drift deeper into it, but at the same time, I am also surrounded by fear and constant chatter. The fear lies in the thought of interaction with others; comfort is when I am alone and I can sleep. When sleeping or just about to sleep, I feel that I have achieved what the day had in store for me; I feel that I have made it across the finishing line once more. It means that I am now finished for one entire day, and therefore, I don't need to see anyone anymore. It is then, at this stage, I feel I have made it through. Successfully or not, just through is enough. Now I can rest in silence. There can be shock tactics or unwanted violations at this time. Feet coming up the stairs can startle me. I'm worried that the owners of the feet may want "to talk." They could be concerned, or they may have a request, something that I need to do. I can sometimes get out of being spoken to and pass it off as me just being tired, or hopefully (and what is the best outcome), the feet coming up the stairs are for someone else in the house.

During the mornings, as I make my way to the station, I drift off into the numbness and think about different scenarios: rolling the car straight into a ditch or just hammering it straight at the big tree that sits at the top of the bend down one of the country lanes. I prefer the ditch option over the tree though. If I hit the ditch, I wouldn't spin back out onto the road. Also, if I were in the ditch and I wasn't totally off the planet after impact, I wouldn't be found as fast as I would be if I was sitting in the middle of the road, which would give me more time, if required, to leave. In addition to the numbness, there's also a constant ranting going on inside my mind. It—the ranting—appears and tells me that I need to do 101 different things, and all of them within the first five seconds of me waking up. Concentrating on any one thing is impossible, and anyway, there's no room for just one thing to concentrate on. All the room I have in my head is being fully taken up by the masses. Due to being constantly under this pressure, I now feel the need to save time and to get on with all these things fast—get it done and get it done now, whatever "it" is. To help save time and speed up getting things done, I've stopped turning on lights when I walk into rooms when at home. I don't want to waste time flicking a switch when I can just shower and clean my teeth in the dark. The thought of wasting time makes me feel ill. I've noticed that I didn't feel like this when we were away the other week, and I think this was because there were older people around looking after everything. When we were away, I had instructions to follow and other people were there who helped by organizing things. I just had to be there and help out when asked. I hadn't needed to be in control of my life as it was being controlled for me. These times, when at home or at work or just alone, are beginning to scare me.

When at work, I now spend more and more time on the fire escape, the empty floors, and the roof. It's at least once a day that I sneak off to be alone. On one of the trips to the roof, I decide who I'll write to. First one will be to my wife; it will be mainly asking for her to not hate me. I'll pen one to the HR lady at the office too. This is just to explain what they need to do with regard to helping my wife get the right insurance pay outs. And that's all. My brother will know why I did what I did, and he'll be upset; but he'll understand, and he'll not need to be told anything that he doesn't already know. He'll then explain this to my sister. Not sure exactly what I'll fully write or say in what will be the final letter to my wife yet, but I do feel some relief as at least I now know who I need to inform.

Back in the City this afternoon, and I have a meeting over by London Bridge station. As I'm currently on Bishopsgate, I think I'll take the bus. It's only a few stops. I'll say about four stops in total. I can see the bus I need. It's currently just up the road from where I am, so I walk to and stand at the stop just outside a restaurant ("With Gez"). As the bus approaches, I put my hand out to signal to the driver to stop as I want to get on. Fucker drives straight passed me!

"Un-Fucking-Believable," I announce to no one as the bus heads off down Bishopsgate. But this is London traffic. The next bus stop is pretty close by plus there are traffic lights in this equation. So I set off and start to chase the arsehole down. Fucking bus drivers. The bus manages to cruise straight through the now-green lights and approaches the next stop where, would you believe it, no one wants on or off. It just keeps going, off toward the bottom of Bishopsgate and the Monument. And so do I; I'm not giving up on this bus. There's no way the bus will make it straight through at the next busy junction. It's a five-way traffic lights—included junction.

I am now gaining on him. As I chase the bus down, people who see me charging toward them move to one side. The ones that don't move, I twist and sidestep. I'm like a Ninja. I'm gaining on the double-decked red fucker with each step. The bus is now at an actual stop, and a few people are getting off. I'm almost upon it; but then the big red git pulls off and carries on, and I'm left with a warm wave of dust from the grille on the side of the bus. It's now at The Monument and Bishopsgate junction, and I have a major decision to make. Up or down? I choose and flee, off down the stairs, through the underpass, and up the other side. I'm breathing like a madman, and my legs are almost total jelly. The steps have taken their toll on me. Shit, I realize that I've come up on the wrong exit. Never mind, I run around the back way and passed The Monument itself and then a quick sharp right brings me onto London Bridge and the penultimate stop on this bus's journey.

Sadly, I miss the bus again. F@#$ it. But there's good news. This bus terminates at London Bridge station, in the actual train station. I decide to leg it over the bridge and catch the red bastard when I get there. A second wind kicks in. I'm Steve Cram. I've slipped it back into fourth, and it's over the bridge I go. As I get south of the river, I skip across Tooley street and then up the slope and into the station. There's a load of poxy buses there now. I wander around searching from bus to bus to bus, and then I see the driver, the fucker. I approach and tap on his window. I'm breathing out of my arse and any other orifice that I have for that matter, but I don't give a shit; this man ignored me, and I'm not having it. He slides his window open.

"You drive pass me at Bishopsgate?" I pant out.

"Sorry what?"

"Did you just drive passed me at Bishops-fucking-gate?"

"No need for the language, but yes. And I'll tell you why."

"You ain't telling me shit. Sitting there all high and fucking mighty. Oooh, I'm a bus driver with my uniform. I don't have to stop if I don't want to. I've got a bus. What have you got?" I rant and shout and gasp for breath all at the same time.

"Look, hang on a minute," he says.

"Hang on? I hung on, you tosser. I hung on at Bishopsgate where you couldn't be arsed to fucking stop. Next time, you might want to think about the small people in the world who just want to use the bus to get to a meeting or shopping or just do whatever they have to do. You tosser." I doubled up on the tosser for this bloke. I then walked off just after the life lesson I had handed out because a police-man started to approach me and I didn't want another argument. As I did walk off, I had a great sense of pride and I felt very pleased with myself. In actual fact, I was fucking elated.

I get to the meeting that I'm supposed to be at on time, and I'm not too disheveled. The company I work for is thinking of bringing in a new system, so I went to take a look at what's on offer and at what cost. I walk into these new, smart, trendy offices. These IT buffs don't work like we do. They're all creative and need to be surrounded by blue walls with clouds painted on them. A solitary plant pot in the corner of an office just doesn't whack it these days. I sit through the presentation, and I conclude that I really like these guys. They're kind, polite, and appear to know what they're talking about but not in an arrogant way. It helps that they are basically normal too. I take the ideas they have and the cost estimate and then head back over London Bridge again on foot. It's back to the City and the Windmill where I've arranged to meet BigFace. You know what is amazing? It's amazing that using a phone in a meeting is frowned upon but using a Blackberry shows that you're multitasking. So during the presen-tation with the IT buffs, toward the end of it, I sent a few mails out to rally the troops for a beer. I have got to tell the lads about the bus driver incident!

"How come you're out early?" says Bigface standing at the bar.

"I had a meeting over London Bridge, and I'm bolloxed if I'm going back to the office."

"Fair enough."

I don't ask Bigface why he's out early; he's never out anything other than early. In fact, he gets annoyed if he has to go back to the office after lunch.

"Anyways," I say. I'm about to tell him all about my efforts in standing up for bus passenger rights. "Have this. I'm standing on Bishopsgate waiting for a bus, just by that restaurant With Gez."

"Aah, that's a pain, isn't it?" he says.

"What is?"

"The bus stop, you know? Not being in use."

"What?" I say.

"The stop has been moved. That one isn't in use."

"What do you mean?" I look at him, confused.

"What do I mean? I mean the BUS. STOP. CAN'T. BE. USED. THERE," he says nice and slowly. "Did you not notice all the scaffolding up?"

"Well, yeah, I saw it, but…" I say and then trail off.

"So…? What happened?"

"Nothing… All well with you?" I ask.

"Yeah, pretty good. I'm popping to the quack's later. Nothing drastic, just need to get my Rockfords checked out."

"Why do I need to know that?"

"You asked how I was."

"Yeah, I did, but I don't want details. You're too graphic. Can't you just say that you've got an appointment?"

"I can," says Bigface. "But then people will always ask me, 'What's the appointment for?' So I may as well just tell them."

"Not always," I say.

"You don't know my mother-in-law."

"Yes, I do, and I'm not her."

We change the subject, and he starts to pry a little. He wants to know about my health, and he's not overly subtle.

"How are you though?" he asks with a face of sincerity and a knowing kind of nod.

"Yeah, I'm well."

"Sure?"

"Yep."

"Any issues?"

I give him a look that says, "Shut the fuck up and leave me alone." It works.

We have similar backgrounds and face similar issues, Bigface and I. My dad drank himself to death, and his mum is currently giving it a fucking good go. We're both able to relate to one another where others who are not in a similar situation can't. I don't pretend to know what he's going through and how he copes with regard to his mum, and he has no idea what I went through with my dad. There are people that think they know how you feel, but they're not you; so it isn't what you feel, and it will never be the same. But for us though, me and Bigface, at least we can compare the nightmare stories that our parents put us through. He's got some real gems, as have I.

The police found his mum once after she had been out on one particularly long session trying to break into a toy shop. She did it, or tried to, so that she could give Bigface a new bike. He's thirty-eight. We both laugh at the absurdity of the situations we are put in. I faced bailiffs, neighbors, and ex-work colleagues, all of which were chasing me up for cash that my dad owed them. Bigface, on the other hand, has his mum chasing him for cash. It's usually cash that he had already put in her account but she had forgotten. She has this remarkable habit of giving her bank card to a "friend," telling them the PIN number, and then forgetting the entire episode. He constantly has to have discussions with her about not handing over her bank card to random people, which she then point-blank denies doing. For me, I would call my dad, he'd slur and forget my name, and then deny he was drunk. It's like top trumps for degenerate parents. I'm still winning this nightmare round though; I have a written-off car and a torched flat. The car...the fucking car. I had nearly forgotten about that.

Now that was a morning to enjoy. It was at a time where Mum had just run off with a new man but hadn't told anyone, and my dad was too ill prepared to accept it. The fact he hadn't seen his wife for two weeks didn't seem to faze him much. He was putting her absence down to her having to work. For two straight weeks? My wife (who was my girlfriend at the time) and I had been out the night before in the area and had stayed over for a night at the family home. In the morning, my dad thought it would be a good idea to "Borry the car, Martin" so he could go and get, low and behold, some beer from the shop. Mum can't drive, and Dad has a work van; so they didn't have a car. Taking a two-ton truck to Spar on a Sunday morning is a bit unnecessary, so he thought he'd help himself and he nabbed mine.

Twenty minutes later there's a banging at the door. Fatbloke, one of the neighbors, is standing at the front door, and he tells me that I had better come round the corner. I do as requested. I arrive at the scene to find that my dad had managed to pull out onto a crossing where he did not have the right of way and was slammed into the side by an oncoming car. The car that hit him was crumpled, and there was debris all over the road. My dad was unhurt and stood there with a look on his face that seemed to say "Bit of a shame that." All this carnage as he'd decided to take my new fucking car, drive the long way to the shops, and not look both ways at an intersection. Now most parents would probably offer up some form of payment or insurance details. Well, he's got neither. The car ended up going to a wrecking yard, and I got the train home. I'm about 15K out of pocket after my insurance pays out. They're a bunch of fucking bandits, insurance companies. All the way home that day on the train, I'm explaining to my girlfriend that she shouldn't worry and that this isn't normal Alberts family activities. She should have probably seen the signs and then run for the fucking hills right then and there.

"Mum's been doing okay recently," Bigface tells me.

"Excellent." We both know this isn't going to last; but we also both know that this is a break, and we need to get them when we can.

"She's got a boyfriend."

"Fucking hell," I say. There's a silence, and I'm about to ask the question. But Bigface continues.

"He seems to want to help her. I mean...he's probably not going to have her eating her five a day and working at a local church. But no money has gone missing from the account, and he limits the amount of vodka she can have a day."

"Fucking hell," I say again. "Are you paying for this care?" We both laugh.

"That's what I thought at first," He says. "It's like a free carer. The problem is..."

"Go on," I say.

"Well, I spoke to my mum, and she said that…well…she's only with him for the sex."

"Ooooh, for fucksake. Bigface, that's rotten." We shake our heads and grin at each other as we acknowledge the bizarre situation. "Aaaah well," I continue, "you'll miss it when it's gone." I'm referring to the drama, not his mother. "Wanna another?"

"Yeah, go on then," he says. Silly question, Bigface always accepts a pint regardless of the time, day, or current pint situation. Today he still has three-quarters of a pint in his hand and has to leave soon, but he'll still take a pint. He always does. Twelve minutes later, he's done the old and the new pint and heads off to the doctor's.

Just after Bigface leaves the pub that afternoon, my wife calls me. "Hi."

"Hi, Bertie, where are you?"

"I'm just finishing up at the Windmill. I'll grab a train in about twenty minutes."

"Okay, everything okay with you?"

"Yeah, you okay?"

"Bertie, I'm fine, but I'm worried."

"What for?"

"For you, for what's going on. You haven't spoken to me in days. You're not the quiet type. I'm worried about you, Bertie."

"'Don't be," I lie. "I'm fine, just tired."

"Is that all it is?" she asks.

"Yeah, of course. Look, I have to go, need to catch the train. And don't worry, I'm fine. See you tonight. Bye."

"Bertie," she says in a kind of a plea.

"Bye." I end the call, and that's that issue diverted.

Walking to the station, I'm thinking, *Fucking hell, this is bad. She's called because she's concerned.* This is the first time that she has called me out blatantly on these possible Wobbles/issues I'm facing. Sneakily, she's hit me unexpectedly. To know that someone cares doesn't help me; instead it makes me fear further interaction with that person. Tonight's going to be a fucking nightmare when I get home. Why won't the world just fuck off and leave me alone. What's the issue with the world wanting to interact with me? What did I do? Right, fuck it, I'm getting a few cans for the train. Good thing about living so far away from the office is that there's a buffet cart. This means that drinking on a train is now acceptable. It doesn't mean that you buy beer from it—that's far too expensive—but you can bring your own and consume it near or at the buffet cart.

When I get home that night, Lazlo has managed to trash a good 65 percent of the house. This is great news! My wife is too tired and stressed with him to be concerned about me. I offer up the option of a takeaway so that neither of us has to cook, and we settle on the seaside classic that's Fish N Chips. This is more great news! Now I can go to the chippy and get out the house, avoiding all interaction. I will go and order dinner, go to the pub whilst it's being made, drink more, get dinner when I feel it's ready, then head home—and all this to avoid further interaction at home. With the food ordered, I head to the Brewsters pub. This is one shockingly weird, oddball local pub. They have beer behind the bar in plastic containers called No. 32 and Steve With the Jumper. The reason for this is because one of these fluids was brewed at No. 32 on the same street as the pub, and the other, I assume, was not brewed by Topless Steve.

There's no one actually behind the bar upon my arrival, but one of the customers gladly stands up and heads behind the bar to actually serve me. There's also a lot of singing going on. Good singing though, not the usual shit. One bloke has a guitar, and he seems to know a load of nineties belters as does a singer who's sitting next to him. They don't seem to take requests, but I can live with nineties covers. This is nice; I like this. There's a fire blazing away in the corner with little concern as to where it spits out the cracking bits of flaming wood or the fumes. The smoking ban hasn't managed to hit this part of world either. My money is on the fact that it never will. I'm an unknown in here; I'm not a full-blown stranger, but I'm no regular either. I'm the guy who works in London. They will possibly know my wife and kids, definitely know anyone whom we know in the village, and have probably heard of us through said folk. "Aaah, yes, you moved into the property up on Redmount way." This is the sort of thing that you hear a lot as a stranger when you venture out into the village; you get encroached upon. They probably know that I threw up on myself. Two swift pints of Guinness later, and it's time to head back to the chip shop to get my order. But there's one thing in the front of my mind that I can't get passed, this one nagging thing that bugs me: "Mr. Chip."

"That chip shop owner's a right arse," I tell my wife as I get back in through the door.

"Why? What's happened now?"

"You know he's got a crap name for his shop."

"Martin, please don't tell me you've had another argument."

"Well, I'm not going back there. Well, I can't go back there actually."

"We have to live here, Martin. We have to see these people all the time. It's not like London. You can't be an arse and get away with it all the time. These people talk to each other. The kids go to the same school. We go to the same shops, bars, and restaurants. I don't want to be the hated family of the village," she says.

"Well, it's not my fault," I say.

"But it is, or it will be. It always is. You called the neighbor a dog on the first day we got here for Christ sakes. Aaah, just tell me what happened." She sighs. She's got me there on the neighbor. I can't refute that.

"Well," I start to labor my argument, "I get in there and get our food, but I can't cope with the shop being called Mr. Chip, so I ask to speak to the manager."

"Really?" my wife says. She has a look of disdain.

"Yes, well, I said to this one guy, 'Are you the manager?' He said no, and then this other bloke said that he was and that it's his shop. So I told him what I thought of the name."

"And what exactly was it that you thought of the name?"

"That it's shit."

"Why can't you just leave things?"

"Where would the world be if we all just left things alone?" I say.

"Don't mock me, Martin. What happened next?"

"I said to him, 'Mate, you've got options: The Cod Father, Frying Squad, Rock 'N' Roe, Chip Chip Hooray, and my personal favourite, Some Plaice Batter. But he just stood there looking at me like there's something wrong with me."

"Can't think why."

"He then said to me, 'What's your point?' My point, I told him, is that with the entire world of shop names relating to fish and chips at your disposal, all you've managed to come up with is Mr. Fucking Chip. It's shit. And then he said to me, 'Are you ordering anything else?' I said not fucking likely, and he said, 'Good. Piss off, you're barred."

"You've been barred from the chip shop. I'm lost for words," My wife said. Whilst I was explaining the event, my wife has laid out some plates, and we sit together for our dinner.

"I am an idiot, aren't I?"

"Very much so," she tells me with a smile. 'So now we just need to never eat fish and chips or see the neighbors. It's not that bad."

"There is always the other neighbor. I've not upset them yet, and there are other chip shops," I add spritely.

Tonight, lying in bed, I have decided to get some help. The way my wife is around me, her understanding, and the way she puts up with such stupidity is all the reassurance I need. It can't go on. I can't go on. No more clouds. I want them to go away. I want the Wobbles to stop. I'm going to get help.

PART 9

DINNER DATE

"I quite like this place," my wife tells me.

"Can I get another large Sapporo, please?" I ask the waiting staff.

We're venturing out tonight. We've risked going into the nearest "big town" from our village on this Friday night. This was once called "going out for dinner," but nowadays it is firmly known as *date night*. When we do go out, we're not overly keen on overtly posh restaurants, and neither is my wallet for that matter. I can't hack paying one hundred quid for a bottle of wine. We went to a very up-market place when we were dating once by mistake. To be fair to us though, the place was called The George, and it looked, on the outside, just like any old pub does. We were hugely mistaken. We walked in The George, and the first thing I noticed was that it was very quiet. People were eating in whispers. Then as soon as the door behind us closed, the maître d' pounced on us and there was no escape. He immediately asked us if we had booked. He could tell this was not our kind of place. I was wearing jeans and a confused face; my wife had a pair of sparkly trousers on. Everyone else in the restaurant was wearing either a suit or a dress.

When I said that we didn't have a reservation, I was praying that they were fully booked. I was ready to turn, leave, and learn the valuable lesson that The George in St Albans isn't the same as The

George on Catford High Street. Unfortunately though, they did have a space and they could fit us in. Sadistic waiter, that's all I needed that night. It was bad news on two major levels. One, this would be an uncomfortable and quiet meal; and two, it was going to cost a fucking fortune. When the maître d' had seated us, he quickly grabbed some menus and then asked if I wanted an aperitif. I felt my wallet shake in fear and my brain hurt as I had not a clue what he meant. Fortunately, my wife took charge of the situation. She's well-educated and unfazed by poshness and snobbery. She tells Sadistic Waiter Boy that we'd both have a gin and tonic and that "My partner would probably like to see the wine menu." Fucking hell. *She's put him in his place,* I thought. *She's nailed it. Class act.* I was absolutely delighted with the outcome, so much so that I wasn't too fussed when I later heard her ordering the lobster.

Luckily for me though, there's now a bundle of new relaxed chain eateries out there, and we're currently sitting in one. It's Japanese, very social and laid-back: long wooden desk-type tables and anyone can sit near you, even if you don't know them! You can also see right into the kitchen where all the chefs are hard at work. I can't help but notice that not a single chef appears to be of Japanese descent.

"Do you have plans for this weekend, Bertie?" my wife asks.

"Nope, I might wander around the village and try to not upset anyone."

"Very funny."

"Why? What are we doing?"

"No plans, I thought it might be nice to have no plans. Maybe we could just have a BBQ or take the boys to play on the green, something like that. It's really mild for this time of year."

This sounds suspiciously like plans to me. "The green will be good. We could have lunch at the pub there," I say.

"Good idea, I'll book us a table then."

That's definitely plans now.

"I'm stuffed." I exhale deeply and stretch backward. "These portions that this place serves up are massive. I can't eat any more." I'm staring at what was once a filled-to-the-brim small bucket of soup filled with noodles, spices, meat, and vegetables.

"Anything to do with the four large Sapporos you've just had?" she says.

"I'll get the bill, unless you want anything else?"

"No, I'm good, thank you. Shall we go to a bar along the high street?"

"Can do."

I gain the attention from one of the waiting staff by using the silent mime when you pretend to draw on your hand to get the bill. She nods, I nod, and the bill is magically on the way without a word.

I start to get out, and then count out, the payment from my wallet.

"Are you paying with vouchers?" my wife asks.

"Yep." There's a confused look on her face for a moment, and then it disappears and is replaced a by a shocked, knowing look.

"Tell me you didn't. Please, Bertie, tell me you didn't."

"Didn't what?" I claim ignorance.

"You know exactly what I mean."

"I don't." I do know, but I'm hoping she leaves it there.

"Did you write to this restaurant chain and tell them that they treated you badly or gave you food poisoning or something like that so that they would send you vouchers for a free meal?"

"Yep," I say and nod, all proud with myself.

"Why?"

"It's free."

"Why did you not tell me before we came out?"

"Because you wouldn't've come out."

"You're not paying with vouchers."

"I am."

"No, no, you're not. What was the story this time anyway? Lactose intolerance, hair in the food, cold food, rude waiter?" she says.

"Racial harassment," I respond.

She looks very shocked at this. My wife's mouth drops. and eyebrows are raised. "No words, Bertie. I have no words."

"What's wrong with that? I wrote to them telling them that I felt unjustly treated, and it could have—not definitely, only could have—been because we were the only black family in the restaurant at the time of the meal."

"We're not black, Bertie."

"They don't know that. That's the beauty of e-mail. It's nonjudgmental."

"You've taken me out for dinner to a restaurant where you were fictitiously harassed whilst eating with your imaginary black family."

"So?"

"Did you make up a name to go with this?"

"Why do you ask?"

"Because I know what you're like. Have you made up an imaginary name for the black version of yourself?"

"Well, Martin Alberts doesn't sound black," I kind of argue the point.

"Oh good god, you have." Elbows on the table, she rests her head in her hands. "Can you come back in a minute, please?" she asks the waiter who's arrived with the bill.

I look down at the floor and mutter the words. "Clinton Ohio."

"Martin, this isn't normal. Clinton Ohio? Why? Oh, for the love—you're paying with your own cash tonight," she says assertively. "You're leaving a big tip, and you're going to give the vouchers to someone who needs them."

"Why?"

"You need to ask why? You're taking advantage of a situation that you've never been in or are ever likely to just for the sake of a free meal."

"These are multi-million-pound companies. They can take the hit."

"Principles, Martin. It's principles."

"Fuck me. All right babe, I'll pay the bill."

"Good, and don't do that again," I get told.

Probably not a good idea to mention that Clinton has already hit up a couple more high-street chains. As we walked to the bar along the high street, we pass by a couple of Big Issue sellers, so I hand over the vouchers so that they can have a free meal. About twenty steps later... "Thanks, Clinton," they call out to me down the road.

It has been a few days since Clinton helped the homeless, and I've decided that before I actually do go to the doctor's, I'm going to try to self-cure. Saying that I will go and then actually going to the doctor's are very far apart from each other in terms of the actual doing part. I haven't had any issues for a few days, and I've been pretty high on life—a bit too much at times, my wife says. She says to me at such times, "Good god, I can't cope when you're like this. It's too much." So with this in mind, I'm getting myself a hobby—something to keep me occupied and engaged in, something that breaks me away from the norm, and something that gives me somewhere that I can go to if and when I'm being "too much." I like to go fishing, but that needs to be arranged and planned. Golf is more a social thing, and if I'm playing bad, then the stress levels go up and the clubs go in the lake. I'll think I'll avoid these activities for now. I'm thinking outside the box on this one.

What's new? What is there that I haven't done before? I decide to wander off, go out and about around the village to plan my new hobby. It's what people do; they go for walks. I quite like wandering around, popping to the greengrocer and the butcher's to see what's in for the day. But not the fishmonger's. He's a first-class arse that man. Someone's upset him once, and he's decided to be a git on the back of it forever. Maybe it was Mr. Chip? Luckily though, there's a guy who parks his boat down by the shore, and he sells what he caught that morning; so I can go to him instead, and he makes his own rollmops. The one downside is that he constantly talks in sexual innuendos, most of which don't make any sense. Does he think that talking this way whilst stinking of fish is a way to get the ladies? I head to him first as it just happens to be in the random direction that I set off in, plus I don't know if I'll buy anything other than rollmops; rollmops I'll definitely be buying. So may as well start there.

"Morning," I say.

"Marnin'," he replies back. It's like talking to the Wurzels down here. His boat is rested up on the stones, and there's quite a lot on display. He's got a good selection today: ling, cod, crabs, lobsters. There's loads. He's also a bit of local hero this guy. He refuses to throw back any dead fish he's caught even if it's over his quota, so he's been all over the local papers as the government keeps on sending him to court. He's been at least four times, but each time the case either gets thrown out or postponed. He keeps all the paper clippings, and he has them up on a sandwich board along with the daily catches and prices. I like it; I like it that he's making a stand against a ridiculous law. I just hope he doesn't end up going down.

"Can I get some ling please and five rollmops? Ling holds together well, right? I can put it in a curry?" I ask.

"Ooooh Ling, yeah. You pop in right in there and give it a good wiggle and it'll be nice and firm for you." He then winks at me.

"I don't want it too hard," I say. God, I'm doing it now!

"Ooh I bet you don't." He winks at me again.

"And the rollmops, please."

"Bet you love a *roll* around," he says, with emphasis on the *roll*.

This statement makes no sense. Where does the coast of England find these people?

"Yeah, don't we all?" I say nervously.

"Twelve pounds, please."

I pay and leave, confused. As I walk off, I can hear him with the next customer who's asking about the crab. "Oooh, a lovely one like you? You don't want no crabs." He laughs out loud.

I realize that I've lost track of the point of my journey. Yes, I want to do some cooking and need stuff to cook, but I need a hobby too. We're in the country by the coast, so it's something outdoors that I'm looking at doing. I do like cooking too…*bang*. I know what to do. I now know what the plan is and what I need to do. I head home, drop off the fish, grab my car, and head to the nearest big DIY shop. I want to get a couple of long beams and some large wooden sheets. I already have a load of tools; so I just need screws, glue, and some outside weather protector for the wood.

In the store, I begin strolling around with a view of what it is I need clear as day in the forefront of my mind. I approach the wood area, and there's a bloke working there with an apron on. Usually, when I am in a DIY store, I always manage to find the staff member who always seems to take some sort of pleasure in me not having a clue in what I'm doing. So I approach with caution.

"Hi, I need some wooden beams please and some wooden large sheets"

"What type do you need?"

"For the long bits, can it be about this big?" I hold my hands together to show him how thick I need it. "For the sheets, about two meters long and a meter across the top."

"Type? What type of wood?" he says back, sounding a bit arsey.

I've just fucking told him what type I need, the long type and the sheet type. What's his problem? We both seem to have hit a cross-roads. This is sooner than normal.

"Hang on," I say to him. I walk around the corner and call my brother.

"All right, mate," my brother says, answering.

"Yeah, look I'm in the DIY shop. I need some wood, and the geezer's being a tool. I need your help. Will you talk to him for me?"

"What are you doing in a DIY shop?"

"I need some wood."

"What type?" he says.

"Don't you start. Some long bits and the sheet-type bits, a few meters long. I've told the geezer this, but he doesn't seem to be grasping what I'm saying."

"I've told you about going to these type of shops on your own," my brother tells me.

"Are you gonna help or just take the piss?"

"What's it for? Is it indoors or outdoors?"

"Outdoors."

"You know the size?"

"Yep."

"Right, just tell him the size you want and ask for aquaplane. I'm guessing the long bits are beams, which you'll cover with the sheets, right?"

"Yep."

"Then the beams can be anything. Just get the cheapest you see, and coat it with a sealant."

"Right. Gotchya. Cheers."

"I'm busy today, mate. So if I don't answer the phone straight away, don't worry. I'll call you back," he tells me.

"I don't need to call you?"

"You will."

"See you later."

"Good luck. Cheers, mate."

I go back to Apron Man and tell him I want one large sheet of aquaplane and I want it cut to a certain size. I also want the cheapest beams they have as they will be sealed and covered by the aquaplane. The material quality of the wood is irrelevant. He cuts the wood, and we place it all on my trolley, which is a bit like a big skateboard.

"Do you need any sealant?" he asks me. I tell him that I don't. I lie. I don't want to be questioned again by Apron Man and his sarcastic demeanor. I sneak around the shop avoiding him and manage to grab the other bits I need. Then I load up the car and head off home and back to garden.

As long I'm out in the garden, not causing any trouble and spending time with the boys who are playing nicely with no sharp implements near them, then my wife will be happy to let me be. We have "no plans" for later when we're actually planning to go to the green and then the pub, but unfortunately, today I am having difficulty interacting with her. I can't speak, so I need a diversion. Today I am not going to be able to talk to her in a nice environment. I am feeling genuinely scared, scared that she will ask me how I am or if there's anything wrong. If she does, I know that I'll either cry or not be able to physically speak. This happens sometimes. I can't talk; I try, but the words will not come out. Today is one of these days. I decide to get on with the job at hand; keep the boys away from the saw, hammer, glue, etc.; and give my wife the afternoon off to go shopping and get her hair cut. It's like a form of deception. I am able to keep the boys safe and fed and get on with my hobby, but I can't speak to my wife; so I need to create a diversion.

On the way back from the DIY shop, I stopped off and went into the hair salon around the corner where I bought and booked a "half head" for my wife for that very afternoon. When I got home, I said to her that I have booked the appointment, "So why don't you go to that and then go shopping after? I can keep an eye on the boys." I managed to say all this whilst looking pretty normal and leaving the hobby in the boot so to not arouse any suspicion. It worked well. I'm now building my hobby, and I'm in a sense of relief; the relief comes from knowing that today I can be alone from all social situations and alone from additional thoughts of bad things. I shall be spending the day with the boys and my hobby and nothing else. The day has been decided; there's not going to be any unexpected additions to it that I didn't know about or want. Later, when my wife gets home, I'll have a bottle of wine and dinner either ready or ordered or I'll be in the middle of the "making of it" stage. Then we can watch a film or anything at all, and then I can go to bed. Sorted. Another day negotiated.

I'm pretty impressed with the build I've managed to put together, and I like the final look. It has taken about three-and-a-half hours, and for a novice, I think it's great. I have surrounded the structure with new turf too. The new area looks like the best part of the garden. I've decided to put a small fence around it to reinstate this area as my dedicated area. Last thing left to do right now is to get the rest of the equipment! So I chuck the boys in the car and set off.

As per my prophecy, when my wife returned from the shops and salon that evening, I had indeed grabbed a bottle—six in fact. I was in the kitchen making dinner, using that ling from the innu-endo-selling fishman. We didn't have to talk as my wife was trying on her new outfits, and when she had finished doing that, I went and bathed the boys. The food was eaten, the film was watched, I claimed that I was tired, and I managed to get off to bed to go to sleep quite early. No footsteps came up the stairs that night, and I slept as best as I could. I want to sleep as much as I can; it helps to turn off the noise. In fact, sleep is all I want to do. But I seem to not be able to do so. I generally wake up around 2:30 AM every day. I stay awake until around 5:30 AM, and then I manage to sleep again until about 7:00 AM unless I have work. During the 2:30 AM to 5:30 AM timeslots I have created, I don't do an awful lot. I mainly spend the time listening to podcasts and sometimes eating. It's not a productive time, but it's not a sad time. I don't feel bad or cry during these three hours. I wander about the house a bit, look in the fridge, stare out the windows, and that's about it. I should probably put this time to better use.

The next morning, I am up and I'm Wobble-free. It is like Bertie 2 has gone away and Bertie 1 is back. Why doesn't it just stay like this? Why do the Wobbles have to come back, always coming back? The fuckers. Alas, I'm up, and with the boys looking on, I am fully absorbed in my new hobby. I've been out already to get extra provisions, and I feel genuinely excited about the new Bertie, the new hobbyist Bertie!

"Morning, want any breakfast?" I ask my wife as she joins us all in the kitchen.

"Tea, please. What are you making?"

"Omelettes," I say, looking smug and deceptive in my mind.

"Oh yes, please."

"Ham, mushroom, peppers, onions? What do you want in it?"

"Ham, cheese, and mushrooms, please."

"Coming up!" I declare.

My wife goes over and sits on the sofa that we have in the kitchen / dining room thingy part of the house, and I bring her a cup of tea. Not a "nice cuppa tea" or a "start the day cuppa tea." Just a normal cup of fucking tea. Tea irritates me. No, actually, tea people irritate me. The times that I have heard someone announce, "I'll put the kettle on," during a time when it is supposed to solve the issue of your dog being run over or your house being burgled makes me fucking sick. Tea ain't fixed shit, and it never will. Get over it and just drink it.

"Ah thanks, Bertie, this is really nice."

"Well, I am a nice person." We both know that's a load of bollocks, but we don't discuss the matter any further.

"Have you seen the news?" my wife asks.

"Only the papers, why?"

"Just that it's the warmest October apparently for quite some time."

"Wanna barbecue today?"

"I was thinking of going away."

"Today?"

"No, just away. Christmas is here soon. You know how hectic it gets. The weather is still nice."

"Although global warming means we're killing our planet," I interject.

"I'm just saying we could enjoy the weather and have a break?"

"I dunno, babe. I can't get much time off at the moment, and I wanted to use what days I have for Crimbo."

"You need a break, Bertie."

"I don't. I'm fine. We'll have a nice Christmas, and I'll be around for all of it."

"Oh my god!" my wife suddenly shouts.

"What?" I say.

"I think…there's a chicken in the garden??" my wife says, peering beyond me and through the French doors. "It must have flown in from somewhere. There's another."

"They haven't flown in. It's my new hobby."

"Chickens are your new hobby? Chickens aren't a hobby?"

"Yes, they are. Anyway, where did you think I got the eggs for your omelette?"

"Oh, I don't know, from a shop? How on earth, where on earth, would chickens be a hobby?"

"Chicken keeping, it's a hobby. I think it is. Anyway, if you want something to be one, then anything can be a hobby."

"There's another. How many did you get?"

"Eleven."

"Eleven? Why would you get so many? What are they going to stay in? Eleven chickens, Martin. We have small children that play in that garden."

"The bloke said you have to have an odd number greater than two to establish the leader otherwise they would all just fight. And he said that if you only have one that it would be lonely."

"Three. Three is more than two and an odd number."

"I've built a coop for them to live in, and there's new grass and a fence. The kids can play outside still. The chickens won't hurt them."

"I'm still on eleven. Why eleven?"

"They had all sorts at the shop, and they were really cheap. They're friendly and sociable too. I just kept seeing different ones and thought I'd get one of these ones and one of those and one of those and so on. There's one out there that looks like its wearing little trousers," I explain.

"Your fence doesn't work."

"Yeah, I'll fix that today."

"What makes you think that chickens are a good idea?"

"Well, we live in the country. I like cooking and going to local shops and things like that."

"That doesn't really make any sense."

"It does to me. And I want a hobby, and they'll not bother you. Wanna meet the girls?"

We go outside, and I show off my handy work. I think she's quietly impressed with my coop. I will need to get the fence a bit higher though; the girls are running all over the garden. I have to turn into Rocky Balboa from the second movie to round them all up and pen them in. I need to then clip their wings and tighten up the security measures. They're all pretty well-behaved and easy to catch, apart from one little bastard who I named Gazza. She's a right handful, and catching her is not as straightforward as it was with the others. Nonetheless, I get her in the end.

A little later, and my handy work is all done. So I go back inside the house.

"I've clipped all the wings so they can't fly off, and I've raised the fence," I tell my wife.

"Good. Look, Bertie, I don't mind having them, but isn't eleven a bit too much?"

"Probably should've got about five in hindsight. I'll take six back next week."

"Can you do that?" she says.

"Yeah, I'll just tell him I can't cope with all of them and that he can keep the money. He just has to take the birds back."

"And do we have anymore hobbies in the pipeline?" she asks.

"Yep, I'm going to start making my own sausages."

PART 10

BLACKPOOL

The next time somebody asks if you'll go on a Stag weekend, make 100 percent certain that you find out where it is and also about the accommodation on offer before you blindly sign up in agreement. A mate of my brother's who has very few friends is getting married. Married, by the way, to one hell of an enormous woman. She's enormous in all possible ways. This in itself isn't that surprising as the UK is a growing nation waist-wise. But when you take into consideration that Paul, the groom in this fiasco, is a muscle-bound fitness freak… well…? Well, it shocks me anyway.

Paul, the Stag, a.k.a. Baldy—he's my brother's mate, they're not very imaginative when it comes to nicknames—at the time of asking me to attend the weekend away had caught me all unawares. I was out with my brother at the time. We were propping up a bar one night after work in the City when his phone goes. We'd been having a few beers in town, and on the end of his phone was this Paul guy. I've known Paul for quite a long time, and when my brother mentions to Paul over the phone that he's out with me, Paul says, "Stick him on." I can hear the loud bastard from just standing next to the phone. I fucking hate that. Not the loudness! I hate it when the phone pass happens. Why, when someone is talking to someone else over the phone, do people feel the need to pass the conversation around to others? No one called me. And I didn't call anyone.

111

But before I could walk off, my brother throws his phone up in the air and towards me, knowing that I'll catch it. Next time, I swear I'll let it drop to the floor. It's a reaction though, sadly, when someone throws something, you instantly catch it. In fact, when we were little, my brother would throw a cactus plant at me and shout, "Catch it!" And I, like an idiot, would do exactly that. He's a bit of a git. Anyway, I then find myself speaking to Paul. He's all jovial, and I'm being polite. Then he says to me down the phone, "You'll be up for the Stag, right?"

And I say, "Yeah, of course."

Shortly after saying that to Paul, I cut him off by means of returning the phone back to my brother. When they stop chatting and my brother hangs up, I look directly in his face and I ask my brother very matter-of-factly, "Did you know he was going to ask me to go on his Stag?"

"I thought he might. He's not got many friends."

"Where is it?"

My brother then pins a whacking great smile to his face and tells me that it's Blackpool.

"You are a git," I tell him.

Ten seconds later, Paul, in what I deem is his excitement, sends me all the details of this glorious weekend direct to my phone. It appears that we're staying at El Riviera B&B! This isn't going to be good. This is going to be shit. I look up from my phone and over at my brother post reading all the glorious details.

"This isn't going to be good."

"What's wrong with it?" he scoffs back at me.

"It's three hundred quid for two nights."

"So?"

"For five of us? Where have you stayed for thirty quid that's ever been a nice place?"

"It's fine. It's got a spa pool."

"For thirty quid?"

"It says it on the text Baldy sent."

"Oh, that's all right then, must be true."

"Why would Baldy make that up?"

"He wouldn't, but the shithole of a hotel that's charging us thirty quid would."

"One more beer before I have to shoot off?" my brother asks.

"Yeah, go on then."

I've had a few things playing on my mind recently, and this Stag weekend isn't going to help. I know that I'll be homesick when I get there. I know that I'll be worried about home, about something that's probably not going to happen, but it'll worry me nonetheless. I'll now have all this additional, made-up worry, all whilst stuck in fucking Blackpool. Fuck, I'm not going to cope with this well. I'm not even there yet.

To add to this, recently I've been shitting a lot of blood. So I probably need to get that looked at, and we know what that means. Those two horrible words as you bring up your knees: "Just relax." My drives to and from the station are becoming something like a shit soap opera. The mornings have me in a state of numbness, and during every single journey to the station, I feel that I am ready to hit my ditch. In the mornings, sometimes, I take a kind of warmth in my dark clouds, and it makes me want to stay in there and never leave. Just stay in the dullness. Of an evening, it's constant tears. I have to pull the car over for five minutes every day before I get back to the house just to wipe the tears from my face, regain some sort of control, and try to look "normal." The other day I actually caught myself crying on the train; this is before I'd even got to the car. It's a good job I live in the UK commuter world as within this commuting day-to-day life there's not a single person that will ever ask you if there's something the matter or stop to help. And I, happily, thank all the fucks in the world for that. I couldn't bear it if someone actually wanted to help, but that's something I don't need to concern myself with. UK commuters don't help others; it's all in the genetic makeup. Don't sit near me, don't talk to me, don't look at me or interact in any way shape or form. I think this is the mantra that all UK commuters conform to.

So with all this shit, all going on daily and with the added small issue of Christmas being around the corner, I'm in a bad place. Christmas worries me; it's a time where I'm going to have to be as normal as I possibly can, all whilst surrounded by people who have actively sought to spend time with me. Still, it's not quite Christmas yet, so for now, let's attack one thing at time. I probably just need to get some rest, and if I do get some, then I'll feel better. Soon, with rest, I'll feel better. I'll definitely be better by Christmas. Onwards and upwards!

The following evening, after the one where I signed up for the Stag do with my brother and Baldy, I find myself on my way to the doctor's. Well, seeing as I was actually referred there by the work nurse, I have to go. I'd had my annual medical at work this afternoon, and for a reason unknown to myself, I had confided that I sometimes shit and leave blood in the pan. It was an off-the-cuff remark, not leading to anything, but the nurse looked shocked. He asked me how long this had been going on for; and when I told him six or so months, he referred me then and there. He said that he could get the office GP to check, but would I prefer the more comfortable surroundings of my local quacks? I opted for the local, not for the comfort. I've never actually been. I don't even know if it is comfy or not. It was a choice I took based more so for the quick getaway from the current situation. Didn't fucking know he'd get me an appointment that night.

I'm standing at the reception desk where the elderly receptionist lady takes my name and date of birth. It's all very quiet in here. I look around at the surroundings and see that there's the token wall that's covered in pamphlets. Are all doctor surgery reception rooms in the UK beige and covered in pamphlets?

"Oh, you're not on our system," the receptionist tells me.

"I've not lived here long."

"Oh, you moved into the property on Redmount Way," she tells me.

"I did."

"Well, you'll need to fill out a form."

I take the form and a seat and get scribbling.

When the buzzer goes ten minutes later, I am summoned to the doctor's office, and I actually feel at great ease. I am totally unconcerned with any nasty outcome. I hand back the form to the receptionist with a smile and a nod and then wander off down the corridor. If something were to be wrong with me, something very wrong, as long as it was quick, I'd be fine. In fact, thinking about it, I could actually just do it—hit the ditch or the roof, do it myself. At least this way, I'd be able to blame "the illness," whatever it is, that is or isn't, actually wrong with me. If I did go into the ditch, with the world knowing I was actually ill, then my family wouldn't hate me; they would understand that I was in pain and struggled to cope with the illness.

"Come in," the doctor calls out after I've knocked.

"Hi, how you doing?" I say upon entering.

"Fine and thanks for asking." He seems genuinely happy. "Do you know that all day I sit in here and I see people and not one of them has asked me how I am?"

"That's the sick for you—self-obsessed pricks. Oh, sorry, doc, didn't mean to use bad language."

"You're fine. I hear a lot worse," he says. "You're new here, according to my records. Either that or you've never been born, ill, needed a jab, etc."

"Yeah, we moved in a few months back, just up on Redmount Way," I tell him whilst pointing vaguely behind me.

"I don't know it. I'm not from the area. I live just outside the county. I'm originally from Bradford but now I'm down here, moved with the wife."

"Sounds familiar," I say. I'm going to like this guy. We bond; I think we're bonding. "Where's all the sick people?" I ask him. "The waiting room is dead."

"It's Friday night," he tells me. "People in this village are usually only ever sick in the mornings."

"Ha, yeah, I've seen them." I laugh. "All of them queuing up right around the corner of the building looking ill, each one trying to look more ill than everyone else. I don't know how you cope with them, doc. I mean, I couldn't. I'd end up telling most of them to just do one."

"Well, it's kind of what we're trained for, what we sign up for."

"Yeah, but some muppet coming in claiming they're about to drop dead with man flu, that must get your goat."

"It has its moments," he tells me.

"How many times a day do you have to say 'Take plenty of fluids, two paracetamol every four hours, and get some rest'?"

He laughs and nods in agreement. At which stage I think he's realized that I'm avoiding talking about why I'm here. "So, Mr. Alberts, what can I do for you?" he says leaning into my preferential line of vision.

"Did you see the referral from the nurse at my office?"

"I have read it, yes," he confirms.

"So we know where we stand and what the issue is," I say.

"When was the last time you passed blood?"

"Fuuuck me, doc," I exclaim loudly.

"Sorry, something the matter?" He looks concerned, shakes his head.

"Yes, there is. Look at the size of your hands! You've got Savaloys for fingers!"

There's a silence in the room for a bit. "Let's get back on point," he tells me.

Good phrase that. I'm going to use that in my next meeting. "Let's get back on point" sounds very assertive and professional.

"OK, sorry," I say. "It happens a lot—once a day-ish, I'd say maybe four-ish times a week."

"And for how long has this been going on? It says here that it has been happening for over six months, is that correct?" he asks me with a concerned look.

"Well, yeeeah…but only recently has it become more often." I try to make a defense for myself.

"Do you think you may have cut anything around the area?"

"I don't go to the arse barbers, doc."

"Okay, I'm going to examine you. You're rather young for anything dangerous, but as it's been going on for some time, I want to make sure."

"Great," I mutter. I climb onto that bed that all doctors have, the one with the paper towel covering it, and lie on my side. I then, as instructed, whip down my slacks and briefs then bring my knees up.

"Would you like anyone else in the room?" the doctor asks.

"Yeah, fuck it. Why don't you call in the receptionist and any spare sick people you can find in reception?"

We both laugh, smirk a little. He understands the humor, and I also think he understands that I'm a little bit afraid. One Savaloy finger inspection later, and I'm off out of there, on my way home. He wants to refer me elsewhere, and I don't care. I'm just happy to be out the room. I'm going to Blackpool tomorrow, and as far as all things are concerned, it's one horrendous episode down, one to go.

"All right, nonce" Fat Bloke's way of saying good morning has always been a wondrous thing. He's got the smallest pointiest head known to man on a not-so-fat body. It's the head size that makes him look fatter than he is. The Stag party has come to pick me up. Fat Bloke's leaning his head out the back window, grinning with excitement. There's five of us in total. Considering that technically I'm a relative of a friend of the Stag, Paul's clutching at straws for buddies. Paul's driving all of us up to Blackpool. He's the driver because he can get company cars. Today he's managed to get a big Mercedes Saloon that we'll all be comfortable in for the journey ahead, plus, as he doesn't drink, Paul driving is a done deal for us and him. Doesn't drink. Not a drop. He stopped drinking over ten years ago and turned to the gym as a replacement for the void. He's got arms like trees, and he always wears the same clothes. Not clothes that would show off his physique, nothing like that at all—just a blue collarless jean shirt, jeans, and desert boots. He's not vain; he's a nice guy and, at times, very funny. I do actually like him. I just don't like Blackpool, among other things. My brother's up front riding shotgun and, in the back, looking normal alongside Fat Bloke, is Side Plate Kris. A quiet guy, a nice guy, a waiter, a clever fucker too. Don't know why he's a waiter. But then, I quite liked the outfit when I had my accident, so I see the perks. Being a waiter is why he's called Side Plate.

"All right, Fat Bloke, how is everyone?" I say.

"Get in the car, you slag. We need some beer. I wanna get there today, and cause you made us drive out to the sticks to get you, you're paying for the beer."

I nod at my brother and climb into the back of the car, then we're on our way to Blackpool. Fat Bloke's constant moaning about me getting the beers in though is already starting to grate on me. We're stopped at some traffic lights after about fifteen minutes into the journey and I see there's an off license. So I dash out the car and into the offie. I grab the first case of beer I can find, pay, and manage to get back in the car whilst it's still sitting at the lights to the delight of everyone. I am quite pleased with myself actually.

"It's not very cold?" says Fat Bloke.

"It's free beer. Suck it up, petal," I tell him.

The journey is the journey. It was never going to be great fun, but it didn't actually take too long. We arrived in Blackpool and at the El Riviera B&B with no beer left and Side Plate's bladder about to explode. I walk into the nonexistent reception and take in the surroundings. If I have ever been to a place that had zero in common with its actual name, this was it. It's basically a terraced house with four floors. Some guy is there, and he wants to know who has the money to pay for the stay; this lucky winner is me. I am then immediately instructed to go through to the back of the building to sort out the payment in the office. I go through, and I'm told by a husky-voiced woman not to let the dogs out as I try to get in to the actual office. This is almost impossible; I have to remove a piece of wood that's blocking the doorway so that I can actually enter the office. I do this and get inside whilst kicking the little dogs backward. Then I replace the wooden board, and we've lost zero dogs.

"Take a seat. Just moved that laundry," she tells me whilst pointing to a bundle of clothes. Fuck me, this is bad. The only chair that's in the office is covered with clothes, which, in turn, are covered in dog hair. And the entire room stinks of stale Rothmans. I move the clothes to the floor, there's nowhere else to put them, and take a seat.

"Right, it's three hundred in total. Cash, please," Shirley tells me—she looks like a Shirley.

"Can I give you two hundred and a cheque or pay by card for the rest?" I ask.

"We don't have a card machine, and I'd rather not cheque. It could bounce."

"The cheque won't bounce. I have a guarantee card, which guarantees the cheque," I tell her.

"Oh, it might, love."

"No, it can't. The guarantee on the card that accompanies the cheques states"—And I point to the card—"five-hundred pound cheque guarantee card."

"We don't usually do that though, love."

"Look, it's fine. It's guaranteed. I just want some cash on the hip. I want to pay by cheque here so that I can spend the cash in your bar."

She seems confused, but after a while, she appears to believe me.

In the end Shirley agrees to take a cheque and fifteen minutes later from dog-dodging, I'm standing in the bar with the lads listening to the barman, who informs us that he is also the manager. He's telling us all about the shithole we've come to. And he seems very pleased with it.

"Good location this. We get a lot of business here."

"Can I park outside all weekend?" Paul asks.

"You can. There's not normally any traffic wardens at weekends."

Sounds legit. I slope away and start to have a look around. God, I'm dreading seeing my room. The bar is a converted living room with two fruit machines and a jukebox. Across the entrance hallway is the restaurant that, oddly, has a pool table in the middle of it. As I look around, I happen to notice that there's a cup of vomit sitting on one of the tables in the restaurant. I see this, and then I also notice that the pool table has a bigger rip in the cloth than the ones that are permanently in Fat Bloke's pants.

Right, we can't avoid it anymore. Let's brave it and go to see our rooms. Rooms, however, being the wrong word I then find out. We get upstairs to face one door. We have one door that opens up to five beds in two rooms. Two of the beds are bunk beds, and as I am the youngest, I get top bunk. Luckily, in the room we also have a broken TV, a damaged wardrobe, stains on the walls, curtains that don't close, and pink scratchy blankets.

"I'm going out," I say.

"Let's have a few here first. The match is on in ten minutes," says Fat Bloke.

"Yeah, go on then. We might as well." My brother, oddly, agrees with him.

"I'll see you downstairs. I need to call my girlfriend," says Side Plate.

The remaining four of us take off down the orange carpeted narrow stairs and head back into the bar.

When I was in our room, however, I noticed something that I wanted to speak to the manager/barman about, and seeing that now we're back and standing at his bar, it seemed a good time to bring it up.

"In the bathroom, there's a sign on the door that says, 'Please make shore you keep the shower door closed…' It says 'shore'?" I tell him.

"Yeah, it's so it don't leak onto floor," he tells me. They don't use *the* up north.

"No," I say. "It says SHORE." And I spell it out, "S-H-O-R-E."

"Yeah, we have to be certain to keep door shut," he replies. "Otherwise water leaks through ceiling."

I just give up at that point. I just nod and say okay.

"It's all right here, in it?" says Fat Bloke.

"No," I reply. "The place is fucking shocking."

The barman then says, "I told 'em when setting up they needed management, but they were like 'Nooo, we'll be fine.' Two weeks later I get the call, and wallop, I'm the manager."

"You've got your work cut out, mate." Paul lets him know. We all turn our backs to the bar and face the TV.

We watched the first half of the match whilst still at the Riviera bar. England are playing and winning against Denmark. Somehow we've decided to remain here for the second half. Well, that was the plan at this moment anyway. During the halftime break, a young northern lad asks us if we would mind if he put the jukebox on. We have no objections. And then BOOM! Drum and fucking bass starts blasting out the speakers. There's only seven of us in the bar and that includes the barman—sorry, manager. We're basically in a front room of a terraced house that not only has fruit machines and poor spelling but the added pleasure of pounding walls and pint glasses that are now jumping along the bar. I've never seen anything quite so inappropriate; it's only two o'clock. Why would he want to hear that shit? And why would he want to hear it so fucking loud? We head out.

Out and about after we leave the B&B, and it has taken us minutes to hit the main area of Blackpool and everything it has to offer and represent. You can't help but notice that the popular look of fashion, which the guys are going for up here, happens to be a black shirt and a white tie. They all look like shit football referees. Then there's karaoke... My good god, there's karaoke. They appear to fucking love it up here. But oddly, these big northern lads don't get up and belt out anything decent. They all start singing ballads? As we're drinking in one of the many bars, a nasty-looking tattooed monster of a man climbs up on stage, mic in hand, and announces he's singing a song by Ronan Keating. It's an odd place here.

After about 8:30 PM, the main bars and clubs are all pretty quiet. This is because everyone's smashed out of their tree by then and have passed out. Some in the street. We end up in a club that looks like a bingo hall, probably is actually. There's about forty-five people in there with us. It's depressing and dank, but it is very spacious... So I guess that's a bonus. I'm standing at the bar getting a round in when I am approached by some lad. He tells me he's having a "Ban-ging tiiime" and that this is "Fookin-grate-place this." He proudly tells me that his friends have all passed out and he's the last one standing. He tells me he's been "on it" for four days straight. He tells me he's called Barry. Barry seems to open up quite a lot, in fact, although I've just met the man. He tells me his job, taxi driver. But not just a driver. He runs a fleet. He's from Manchester, has four kids with different mothers, hates his own dad who ran off, and he once knocked "clean spark owt" and that he's a "top, top deejay." Barry then asks me if he can hang around with me and my mates. The last thing I want is another friend on this trip. So I tell him, "Yeah, sure. Go and see my brother. He's just over there. Go and introduce yourself, and I'll bring over the beers." I stand back and watch. This geezer, Barry, walks over to my brother and does as I instructed. I can't hear the conversation, but I can see what's happening. After the guy stops talking, he offers his hand up to shake with my brother. My brother looks him up and down, hands at his side, and mouths the words "FUCK OFF."

The next day and a half in the Vegas of the North are long. They really, really drag. The only good part being that there wasn't any deaths and I did finally get home. Fucking hate Blackpool.

PART 11

CHRISTMAS

I've written and sealed the letters. I've left them where they can't be found for the moment. I'll move them to a more prevalent location when the time's right. I've made the decision that I'm not going to do anything during Christmas though. Even I'm not that much of an arse. Leaving a family with the nagging, dreading thought of Christmas every single year because that was when their brother, mother, uncle, or whoever it was topped themselves is just a bridge a bit too far. At the moment though, I happen to feel rancid and ill, too ill to move. Not my normal ill, I feel sick and tired and I have a fever. So it seems that I'm just that bit too ill to pop off at the moment. Shame actually, to be ill, at this time of year with all the people planning to visit. I had been totally fine before today in fact. We had even managed to have that short break, the break that my wife asked about going on two months back.

We went to the house in France, and I did a bit of skiing. It was my first time skiing, and luckily, I was a natural, sort of. My wife has skied loads, has done since her teens, and is very capable on the slopes. The place where we went to, for my debut, was great, is great. It's a small and very cheap location which is only ever used by locals. No tourists go there; they don't know anything about it. Well, we do, but apart from us the people that go there to ski all live locally. They take their homemade lunches with them, park up, ski for a bit, and then stop and all have an outdoor winter picnic. It has a real family feel about the place. For me though, more than anything, it's a safe place, just a safe place for me. I felt so very happy and relaxed there.

In the morning when we're there, we drive up the mountain from the house and just before we get to the slopes, we hire the boots and the batons we need along with a set of skis for my wife. I don't need to hire skis as I borrowed some from a mate who was too short for them. We get all this stuff from the village where we also buy a ticket so that we can ski for the afternoon. The cost is minimal, which is another thing I like about it.

On the slopes the selection is small but fun. The place only has six runs, three of which are black runs, which my wife says I'm not allowed to go down. Whilst at the base and to get to any of the runs, you need to get transferred via an amazing contraption called a button lift. These lifts are like the old rope swings we used to hang off as we went flying over the rivers in the council estate parks. What you need to do is grab the pole and shove the seat between your legs, but you don't sit. These are wise words: do not try to sit. I tried to sit first time and fell off. My wife had already told me that I would fall off. She had said that a few times, but I refused to believe her until it happened. She said to me not to worry about falling off, everyone does on their first time. She said this to me in queue, and then she whooshed up the mountain on the lift.

I brushed all the comments to one side, grabbed the pole, sat on the seat—or as it is known, the button—and then as the lift jerked forward, I fell off it and landed on my arse. My wife, at that stage, was out in front and already halfway up the slope. The French guys there were great. They picked me up and dusted off the snow, then after a few minutes of them realizing that my French is awful, they lined me up for another go at navigating the demon button lift. This time, however, I was ready—ready to not sit and ready for the jerking motion. I took hold of the lift's pole, straddled the button, and *wallop!* I was off and running, heading up to the mountain summit. I was halfway up when I noticed my wife gliding down over on the other side of the slope. I called and waved with great excitement and an element of pride. My wife saw me, stopped midway down the run, and started to sidestep back up the mountain so we could meet at the top. I think she felt the need to help me get down the slope as this was my first time. So with this in mind, I waited at the top for her.

When my wife finally arrived at the top, I was ready to bolt. I crouched down, had tucked in my chin, and gripped the batons under my arms, looking to remain low and aerodynamic for total speed. Speed was my goal. I will be speed itself. My wife looked at me with confusion, pointed out that I was not Alberto Tomba, and to stand my arse up. We all had a really great time there. The kids loved the snow, and we were away from everything and everyone. It was pretty peaceful, and no one had any Wobbles or troubles. But now back in the UK, Christmas is about to hit and I'm laid up sick. My wife currently has a million things that need doing, and I'm just not up to the task. And me being sick isn't going down well at all. My wife will openly admit that she hates it when I'm ill. As I lie on the sofa, I do my best to try to be invisible. I can feel tensions in the home. I'm not in anyone's way, but I can't be ill now, not with the in-laws on the way. Not with Christmas.

"Martin, are you going to get up and move today?" she asks.

"Babe, I'm really ill. I'm not joking."

"God, I hate it when you're ill."

"I know, I'll get everything done later or tomorrow. I just need to sleep for a bit."

"Tomorrow's Sunday," my wife points out.

"So? Shops are open. It's Christmas."

"Monday is Christmas Eve." Again she's pointed out to me the days. She knows I wasn't sure. I did actually think Christmas Eve was Tuesday though, so it's a fair statement.

"Okay, look, don't worry. I'll be fine by tonight. Oscar had this. It only lasted a day. Just let me rest, and then I'll be back in the game by tonight/tomorrow."

"Well, you're not staying there, lazing around on your arse all day and watching sport." It's a known fact that you can't be ill and watch sport at the same time, not in my house.

About an hour or so passes, and I'm still in the same spot on the sofa; but I also have a bowl with me as I think I may puke at any moment. Oscar is watching kids' TV with me, and Lazlo is around somewhere, probably breaking things. He really is one angry kid. I remember coming home once after popping to the shop, and he was going crazy because he'd lost a card game he was playing with his nan and granddad! I had to carry him to his room, shut him in, and then hold the door closed tight like some sort of prison cell barricade, all whilst he was on the other side kicking and throwing things at it. I remember calling down the stairs, "Who let him play cards? You know what he's like if he loses at cards." My guts have started to tighten, and there's that feeling I know only too well. I grab the bowl that I placed next to me by the sofa, and then I hurl up the watery contents of what I've managed to eat over the past twenty-four hours, which isn't much. Just as I'm doing this, my wife enters the room. There's nothing but a look of disgust on her face.

"Oh great. Well, that's that salad bowl ruined," she says.
The rest of the day I'm laid up I'm sitting with Oscar watching a bundle of kids shows. He likes this one show about a fireman who lives in a small village.
"Big Guns, why isn't that ginger kid arrested? All he does is cause total mayhem in that town," I ask. I nicknamed Oscar "Big Guns" when he was born as he was pretty big, even though he was premature and not very well. He was so big that he could just about squeeze into that incubator thingy that kept him safe.
"I don't know, Daddy."
"Well, they should at least give him an ASBO."
"What's a ASBO?" he asks me.
"It's what naughty kids get to stop them from being naughty."
"Has Lazlo a ASBO?"
"Not yet. Can we watch something else?"

"Robot in the skies?" he says. He means *Transformers: Robots in Disguise*, but I'm not going to correct a three-year-old. I'm also not going to watch it either.

"Nah, it's rubbish. What about Woody Buzz?"

"Okay."

Woody Buzz is *Toy Story*. He's very agreeable is our Big Guns; he's nice and accepting. Lazlo, not so much.

Next morning I get up, and I'm feeling physically much, much better indeed. The in-laws are now in town, and we're all getting ready for Christmas Day. But however, my wife is now ill. And I can't help but think to myself, *Ha, that's how it feels*. I'm slightly, genuinely, fucking delighted that she's now got this bug, and I fully intend to be overly nice and kind to her. I'm going to be so kind that it's going to make her want to vomit. Which is very likely, seeing as this bug thing has done exactly that to me and Big Guns over the last couple of days.

"Stay in bed, babe. I'll do everything, don't you worry. I'll get to the shops for what we need, and I'll drop off all the presents at the same time. You just rest. It's awful, isn't it? Feeling like this. Can I get you some soup or paracetamol or water?" I offer up in a sincere voice. I'm a regular Florence fucking Nightingale.

With my wife in bed and chores to do, I plan on offloading Lazlo with any relative I can find and take Big Guns out with me to save Christmas. Lazlo's not in best of moods today, and we've already had an angry shouting matching over a book. The book in question happened to have had a walrus in it, but Lazlo was insistent that it wasn't a walrus, and in fact, it was a seal. It fucking wasn't, but he wouldn't have it. "No walrus, seal," he kept shouting at me. Granted, they are similar; but this had tusks, and it actually said walrus on the page right fucking underneath the picture. He wasn't having any of it and just kept interrupting me and telling me I was wrong, so we couldn't get past the page. It was stalemate. In the end, and with jobs to do, I had to take the moral high ground. So I said to him, "Okay, whatever, you're wrong. You can't even read yet anyway, so be wrong.

And when the time comes, people at school will laugh at you." He seemed happy with the agreement. To be fair, with my wife being ill, the last thing she really needs at the start of the day with family around is for me and Lazlo going at it; hence, I diffused the situation.

Watching the news that morning on the TV, there was a report where they mentioned that if you were feeling sick, you should NOT go to the hospital or the doctor's surgery. Apparently, there's an outbreak of a virus called the Norovirus!!! It will last a couple of days, and when you get it, you'll feel like shit and throw up, words to that effect. If you come to the hospital, they can't help you, and you're only going to spread the virus. So stay indoors and rest. Blimey, that's what we've had, what we still have. I run upstairs and into the bedroom to see my wife.

"I know what wrong with you," I tell my wife. "You've got the Norovirus. It's on the news. It's wiping out East Anglia. Don't leave the house, or you'll spread it. And don't go to the doctor's, that's the official line."

"Okay," she says. Is that it? She doesn't look very interested in my ground-breaking news and classification of her symptoms. I'm a bit disappointed. It's probably cause she feels so shitty; she'll be more enthusiastic later, tomorrow. I'm sure.

"Right," I tell her. "I'm gonna drop Lazlo off with your mum and dad, then get all the gumpf. I'll see you later."

I've never had a famous virus before; I now feel a bit famous. I should probably call the news station and report myself as a survivor; they might want to interview me. Best get the shopping first though. So I run the boys over to where my mother-and father-in-law are staying. They've hired a barn in the village for the festivities. As I get there, I'm greeted at the door by my father-in-law.

"Hi, you okay to keep Lazlo for a bit? I need to get all the shopping done. I'll keep Big Guns with me. Missus is sick. She's got the Norovirus. It's famous. It's on the news. I've had it already, but I've come through the other end, literally—well, both ends in fact."

"Yes, of course, sure. Do you need anything from us?" he asks.

"Nah, I'm good. I'm fit and ready to save Christmas. It's Christmas Eve tomorrow, so no time to waste. I won't be too long. Buzz me if he kicks off and you need rescuing. Don't play cards with him, nor should you read books on ocean wildlife. See ya."

"Okay, Martin, we'll be fine. See you later."

I wrestle Big Guns back into his car seat. He's getting ever bigger, and the straps must chafe by now. But seeing as I've got a shopping list that would make you think there's at least seventy-five people coming to dinner, I need to crack on; there's no time to waste.

After spending a lifetime trying to park, Me and Big Guns finally get into the main area of the shopping town, the high street! And now we're ready to attack the list. Just then, my phone goes. It's Smudger.

"You arsehole," he says. Doesn't even give me a second to say hello.

"And a very good morning to you, Smudge."

"You fucking git."

"All right calm down. What's got you all twisted? Oh, is it the Norovirus?"

"I can't believe what you've done, and no, I don't have the Norovirus. What is that anyway?"

"It's a famous virus. It's been on the news. I'm a survivor."

"Stop changing the subject."

"I don't know what the subject is Smudge, other than you calling me names."

"All the lads at the club, including my own brother, think that I'm the Lakeside Shopping Center Father Christmas."

"Why would they think that?" I ask.

"Because you started the rumour."

I had actually forgotten all about that, one of my finer moments I feel.

"I got ripped apart by everyone at the club yesterday," Smudge continues. "They were saying things like, was I doing it to spend time with kids? Or is it that I'm just hard up for cash. They took me apart. I got humiliated."

"Brilliant." I half laugh back to him down the phone. I'm mean, fuck me. He doesn't half moan. Can't he see the genius element here?

"Such an arse, Bertie."

Clearly not then.

"Anything else?" I ask.

"Wanker."

"I'll see you in the new year, Santa," I tell him.

"Tosser." That's the last word I hear as he cuts me off. I'll call the lads later and bask in my glory, but for now, I have a task to complete: I shall save Christmas.

I'm already slightly ahead of the game here. En route into town, I managed to drop off all the gifts my wife had bought and wrapped for the family members and friends who live nearby to us. I say friends loosely; there was stuff in that load for people who are basically getting a gift for going to work. There was a gift for the nursery teacher and a gift for the lollypop lady? Plus a gift for the neighbours? Granted the neighbour gift is probably on the back of the "dog" comment. There was also a gift for a family, an entire family…? I assume this is all because we once turned up to a party for one of their kids??? There's a time for giving, I get that; but it seems there's also a time for spunking cash up the wall on a load of random people. Alas, time is running low, and I have a mission. Right now it is time for the list, and knowing that the Smudger windup has gone very well, I'll acquire everything with a smile on my face and a skip in my step. Onwards and Upwards!

A few hours later, Big Guns and I have managed to get everything that was on the shopping list. Big Guns hasn't been of much help, in fact; give him a sausage roll and a banana, and he's the easiest kid on the planet. With the list though, most of it had been preordered, so luckily, I just showed up, paid, and then collected whatever it was. The Butchers and the greengrocers had all the stuff ready for me. Pretty handy. In actual fact, the Butchers were quite protective of my items. It turned out that some rouge turkey shopper had apparently rocked up and tried to claim my bird! But this rogue was met with a "You're not Mrs. Alberts" by the angrier one of the butchers and was ushered away out from the shop. When I got there to claim my bird, the butchers seemed please that they'd guarded it, told me all about it; but they were also disappointed that it wasn't Mrs. Alberts who'd come to collect and that it was me. I think they were looking forward to seeing her. One butcher had a bow tie on?

Big Guns, my good self, and four hundred bags of shopping later, we jump in the car and we travel back over to the barn where the in-laws are staying. I think the plan is that when back at the barn, we're having drinks and some dinner and probably bask in the praise of me saving Christmas…?? Probably not. Anyway, I'm starving. I've not eaten for two days, which is mainly due to the fear of seeing it again. But now I'm so hungry that I am willing to risk that factor. On the way back to the barn, I spoke to my wife, and I find that she is still ill; so she has to stay on lockdown back at ours. There's no option. We, the healthy people, all agree that we don't need this virus spreading any further. Also, as we're having Christmas dinner at the barn, I can dump off and leave all the shopping here. My plan now: eat, drink, be merry, and I'll come back in the morning to start peeling the veg.

"Hi, Martin, how is everyone?" My mother in-law asks me just as I click the lock and enter the barn with Big Guns under one arm.

"Good thanks. I'm Hank Marvin. I've got all the stuff though," I say to her, looking and feeling pretty proud.

"I was referring to my daughter?"

"Ah yeah, she'll be fine. It's just a twenty-four hour thing, I'm sure. Not been home yet though. Me and Big Guns have been saving Christmas. Lazlo behaved himself?"

"He's an absolute angel. He's been lovely all day."

I nod and smile. Yeah, he's an angel all right, hell's angel. Lazlo and I then exchange looks.

"I did try to get the turkey, to help out," she says. "But the butcher told me to go away and that I was not Mrs. Alberts."

"Hhmmm, yeah. They can be a bit protective of their poultry round here."

After dinner, I say bye to the in-laws and put both the boys in their car seats, ready to head back to our house. It's immediate. The feeling. As I shut the back door of the car, it felt like a trigger or a switch. Just as I put the boys in their places, left them, closed their doors, and walked around to the front of the car. I am now alone; it's not for a long time. I'm just walking around the car toward the driver's seat, but physically alone for a moment. In a gravel drive, in a field, clear black skies, cold air—I'm alone. I'm away from all the grown-up people, and within a second, a dark cloud has covered me. Numbness and sadness has hit out of nowhere. Fuck off, fuck off, fuck off, not now, go the fuck away. I'm not feeling this way now, not now. Why should I? I try to shake it off. There's nothing to be concerned with, everything is done and everything is all set. We are all here and everyone's happy, so just fuck off.

Then I start to cry. Oh fuck me, not now. Will it just stop? Why the tears? I get in the car and start up the engine. I've only got to drive ten minutes around the corner, but I can barely get out of the grounds that surround the barn because I can't see properly with all the tears. But I need to move. I don't need my in-laws coming out to check on why it's taking so long to leave the parking area. Good god, I don't want this dread, not now. I just don't want it anymore. Things were going well today? Why has it happened now? It's too late though. It's now in and it's settled. The Wobble has just checked in for a stay at Hotel Bertie, and this is now going to need hiding from the whole world for God knows how long. I look behind me at the boys. They're happy; they're so happy and carefree. Both boys have no idea what a full-blown fuckup they have as a father. Or maybe they do? What if they know? If they don't, what's going to happen when they find out (if they haven't already)? This is something I cannot let happen. How could I ever tell my own kids that if they are in trouble and need help or support that I'm not going to be able to help them? I'm a total fucking mess inside and out.

I drive around for a while. As the boys are now fast asleep in the back, I've decided to stay in the car too and take a route out of the village and into countryside obscurity. Once the initial shock of sadness and the tears pass, I just slip down and sink into the numbing state of this particular Wobble. It starts to feel like the correct place to be. If I stay like this, then I'll just be silent. I'll not trouble anyone. I'll just keep myself to myself and remain aloof, away from everyone; they just need to leave me alone too. I'll remain in this distant state until the latest time possible when I will eventually have to play a part in human interaction. I've been driving around for at least an hour. I haven't stopped anywhere, and I'm not sure where I've been or what's been playing on the radio. I should get back, get the boys home. My wife may have spoken to the in-laws; they'll say I left at whatever time it was, and that leaves me open to questions, interaction. That's what I don't need right now.

After returning home and putting the boys to bed, I get stuck into the fridge, which is full of Guinness. I say fridge, but it's actually the garden shed. All the beer sits out in the garden during the winter. I quite like keeping my beer outside; the chickens aren't going to drain it, and it leaves room in the fridge for food. The main bonus though is that I get to walk away from any situation that I don't like just by using the excuse that I need to go and get beer from the end of the garden. Tonight I decide to stay for a while though, sitting in the shed and not moving, just looking out the window and into the garden. It's fucking freezing in there; but I'm wrapped up in my ski coat, and I have my large black mittens on, which, luckily, have a rubber outer lining making it easy to hold my beer. My house is looking very quiet from here, and no one seems to be looking for me. I can safely stay here for a while. Not sure why I chose here. The shed is full of crap, and the only thing to sit on is a metal trunk, which will probably give me farmers. It feels like the right place to be. This will pass, this one, this will pass. I'll be better in the morning. I just need some sleep and a shower. Tomorrow is Christmas Eve, so I just need to get through to Boxing Day. That's when most of the people will be heading off elsewhere, so it's just the two days really. It'll be fine. This will pass.

I sink four or five beers whilst rocking back n forth on the trunk. Getting up, standing, I decide it's now time to get my frozen arse cheeks out of the shed; and so I go to see and check on the chickens. Well, the five I have left. I returned the others with a cash and food contribution back to the original farm. The owner seemed happy. Well, he could hardly be angry. He sold his birds for three days and got them back with a bag of feed and some bonus cash as well as the initial sale price. My birds are all present and correct; no one has escaped. They're happy too. I know this as sad hens don't lay eggs, and these feathered delighted ladies are dropping constantly. I check their feed, water, and see that they have enough straw. I'd be a chicken in my garden; it's a good life. All you need is right there for you. I wander around the garden for a while longer before going back inside. Inside the shed I'm not ready to go inside the house yet. I'm fine where I am for now; I'll go back in the house and up to bed in a bit. My cheeks can endure a bit more.

I wake up in my bed the next morning, and I feel a massive pang of guilty stress that's totally engulfing me. Where the fuck has this come from? This wasn't there last night? My phone then rings almost instantly from being awake. Am I being watched? It's the father-in-law. He tells me that his wife is sick. Looks like she's got the Norovirus and that it's just a matter of time until he gets it. Probably. I think they think that this is my fault? It sounds that way. Them being ill is now adding to the stress that I've somehow managed to on board overnight in my sleep. My hands have started shaking, and I'm sweating. For fuck's sake, all I've done is move from horizontal to an upright sitting position in my bed. It's only 10:00 AM; this day is shit already. I used to love Christmas Eve, but if this one well and truly ended right now, I'd not miss it for a moment. I should lie back down and relax. No, not now. Now's the time to get up. Right, I need to front up, shake this shit off, and get the fuck on with my day. I'll get up and get on with the day, and I'll rest up later when the day's over. Just need to get through till then.

Downstairs, my wife's back on her feet and looking gorgeous. How does that work? I don't know. She's putting up with a lot, I guess. I mean my behaviour might be affecting her. If she knows that anything's wrong, that is. I don't think she does though, plus I don't have time to worry about people worrying about me. I need to be worried that they don't. A deep breath and smile and I enter the morning's first phase of interaction.

"Feeling better?" I ask.

"So much better. I felt terrible yesterday. Thanks for helping out and looking after me." I almost cry at her genuine kind face that's being thankful for my efforts.

"Don't worry about it, anytime. Oh and I got a new salad bowl yesterday whilst out." We both smile at each other, and I start to lose the guilty feeling. She's making me better by smiling and not thinking that I am the usual reckless idiot that I am on most days. My wife manages to help subside the shittyness of these Wobbles with some kind of mystical magic. I grab some coffee from the disc machine thingy that sits on the kitchen worktop. You can get loads of different flavours from all over the world for it. Today I opt for a Columbian roasted matured blend. Nescafe granules would do; but hey ho, I've got the machine, so I'm using it. Standing with my tiny cup that makes me look like a giant in hand, I turn to my wife. "Your mum's sick. Your dad's just called."

"Oh no, this bug is awful. It's wiping out everyone, Martin."

"Yeah, it's bad. What should we do? I mean, do we go round or not?"

"Well, we've had the bug, so we should be fine. We can't not go and see them. It is Christmas Eve, and we've planned it."

"What if I get it again?" I don't fancy blowing chunks all day on Christmas Day.

"That's a risk you'll have to take, Martin. We'll leave in an hour."

"Hmmm." I nod back in agreement. I'm not sure about this. I mean Christmas Day—the day you get drunk twice. I don't want to spend it with my head down the toilet. That's what Boxing Day is for.

After breakfast and my tiny coffee, we head over to the barn where I am greeted at the door by not only my father-in-law but he's also brought with him a disapproving look. I choose to ignore it. I slide, sidestep past him, and I then choose to go straight into the kitchen and to get to work on the mountain of vegetables that need peeling and prepping for tomorrow. Thank fuck for sprouts. These nasty, stinky little green bastards have got me tied up for hours. After my wife and father-in-law exchange pleasantries and concerns for one another's health, my father-in-law joins me with the veg challenge, and oddly all seems well? I'm confused. I seem to have misjudged the situation. People are upset because they are sick, but they're not upset with me. They're just upset; there's no blame! This feels like a real relief. The slightest bit of reassurance that I can get will go a very long way today. My father-in-law puts his hand on my shoulder and jokingly says, "Oi, I'm on sprout detail. You're getting the potatoes."

I take in a large gulp. I nod, smile, and try to crack a laugh. "Fair enough. Just need to pop to the bathroom, then I'll get straight onto it," I tell him. I dash upstairs, into the bathroom, and burst into tears. That moment, the hand on my shoulder, it's what I crave; it's what I need. It's a simple fucking hand on my fucking shoulder, and I'm now in the bathroom pissing out of my eyes. What the fuck is happening? It's Christmas Eve. I'm surrounded by people who care and are happy, albeit a bit sicky. This should be—and it is—a nice time. I shouldn't be hiding in here crying. I should be enjoying the time. That's what I should be doing.

Right, fuck this for a game of soldiers. Get yourself together, Bertie, and man the fuck up—you've got spuds to peel! A deep breath or two later and a wash of my face, I'm back downstairs standing side by side with my father-in-law, up to our elbows in vegetable peelings. I think we both like the job aspect of the day; we're not good at doing nothing, and we both need a purpose.

"Oi. Don't chuck them in the bin!" I say this to him just as he's about to launch a mountain of sprout leaves into the rubbish.

"Why? What are you going to do with them?"

"I'll give 'em to the girls."

"Girls?"

"Yeah, the chickens."

"Chickens?"

"Best not bring it up too much at the moment. It's a bit of a sore subject," I tell him. He nods and understands, but I think he's interested and wants to meet them. "I'll introduce you to them soon," I tell him. "Just keep all the veg cuttings for now. There's a bundle of free eggs in it for you'.

The veg is all prepped by the early afternoon, and tomorrow is now looking in good order, preparation-wise. We all just need to not vomit anywhere, and hopefully, we should all have a good time. I've also just decided that later this evening, I'm going to go to midnight mass. I've not been before, and I think that it'll be nice. So I'm going to go.

"Babe, I'm going to midnight mass later," I announce.

"Okay, any reason why?" she asks confusedly.

"I've not been before, and I think it will be nice. You don't have to come."

"Okay, well, we'll be back at our house, and the boys will be in bed by then. So you can wander round to the church if and when you want to go."

"I do want to go."

"Okay."

When I do get to the church for midnight mass, I can't actually fucking believe it, but it's already started? Surely midnight mass means get there for midnight? Nope. I walk in, and they're already up and running. The vicar is up front chatting away. It didn't help that the door's a right noisy bastard, too, so I've managed to make sure that everyone in there now knows that there's a latecomer who's just arrived. I enter at the very back of the church, and it is rammed, packed out, sold out, looks like standing room only. Eveyone's now looking at me, and they usher me forward. I walk forward slowly, with an "excuse me" kind of look on my face. I can't find a place to sit though. To get a seat on a pew, I have to walk right down the middle aisle. It's like I'm about to get married, and it's all eyes on me. I'm only looking for a poxy seat. I can't turn around and leave, not now, although it's the only thing I want to do. I wish that they would just stop watching me. I can't turn around, so I just keep walking forward, hoping someone will get up or shift along a bit; but no one does? Where's the Christmas spirit in this place? In a couple more steps time, I'll be up with the vicar. Why is no one helping me here? I'm getting dangerously close to the front. I'm now at the fucking front. I'm in everyone's plain sight. The vicar is still reading a story, and I look like some drongo who's in the wrong building. Maybe I should kneel down at the front ledge bit? I don't know what the protocol is. I'll bow, that's a sign of respect. Just then, someone dressed in a white robe taps me on the shoulder and points to a space at the end of the pew to my right. It's at the very front of all the rows on the far right next to the wall. I take white robe man up on the offer and go and sit down. This is prime seating. I can see the whole show from here. Result!

This is very Christmassy. I mean this is really very, very Christmassy. I bet that I even recognise the songs. The vicar continues his story and talks to us about lost ones, and I can't help but think of Dad, the useless drunk that he was. I never felt inspired by him, nor did I really respect him, but I did like him. He was a pain in the arse and financially damning, but as a guy in the pub or a bloke who loved his kids and was proud of them, he was a good egg. Lo and behold, the tears start to come. These, however, are not the usual tears; these tears are welcome. This feels like a release, some kind of excess release, or that a type of damage that's been living inside is now leaving the body. I'm genuinely happy to have these ones. I'm smiling and crying; and I feel genuinely, oddly, happy. Don't know anyone here, don't care either; I feel safe to show my emotion, my current emotion, how I feel now. I get right into this mass. I'm right slap bang 100 percent into this. I sing along with the next song too. I fucking knew that I would know one. Oh coooooome oh ye faaaaaithful! The way I feel right now, if they do Jerusalem, I'll be the British Pavarotti.

There's a bit in church when you shake the hands of people near you. You shake them and say something like "Be in peace" or "Peace be with you" I think it is. When I was in cubs, I hated that bit. I didn't like the idea of talking to and shaking the hand of a stranger. Tonight, or this morning to be more accurate, an elderly lady who's sitting behind me taps me on the shoulder. As I turn around to face her, she takes my hands. She seems to know that something is not as it should be. She looks at me and says nothing; she just smiles. I don't think I know her; I'm pretty sure I don't. Maybe she's just a kind soul, and she wants to let me know? Either that or I've just pulled, in church! The white robe lot then call my bench up to the front. I don't really wish to go; I'm not sure what it is that I am supposed to do if I go anyway. The guy to my left eagerly tries to coerce me forward, but I refrain. And then my lady friend puts her arm between me and him, like a force field. He gets the message and leaves me alone. After the bit where they've all gone up to the front, we have one more song, a prayer, and we are then encouraged to hang around at the back for tea and coffee. I don't hang about though. I've had my church fix, and it's now time to leave. As I leave, I feel immense. I'm ready for Crimbo. It's a given. I'll smash it this year. *Boom, bang* and *boom* and *bang!*

As I get home, I see my wife on the sofa with Lazlo asleep in her arms. I assume he's been his usual self.

"He's broken the side clean off from his cot, and then he kicked the stairgate off the wall." My wife looks down at him with a loving, painstaking smile whilst telling me the news.

"Kicked it off? Off the wall?"

"Yes, off the wall and down the stairs."

"Blimey, that's not normal," I say.

"I've put some suitcases at the top of the stairs for now. It's all I could think of. To block Oscar, so he doesn't fall down the stairs. Lazlo will have to sleep down here with you until it's fixed."

"Why do I have to sleep with a nutcase?"

"I've been asking myself that, Martin."

"Never mind all that. Church was well good, apart from the weird bit when you have to shake hands. Why do they wanna do that? Just reach to a stranger and hold hands in an odd way?"

"I don't know, Martin. Maybe to show that they care?"

"Hhhmm, you may be right there."

Christmas Day went without any issues. Apart from the father-in-law getting the bug and being laid up for the day. There were no arguments at the dinner table whilst wearing silly hats, no drunk relatives being abusive, kids enjoying the spectacle, and no major breakdowns by me. A decent Christmas.

I fucking love Boxing Day. I always have. Well, to some extent. When I was a kid, the good side of my family would visit us on Boxing Day, meaning good times and genuine fun. That all went south though when Mum ran off. Alas, said times are back! As an adult and now living here in this village, I enjoy Boxing Day again as much as I did before. Now, this is either because the storm has left that was Christmas or that there's a party tonight? Today's got both though, a double whammy. So with all this in mind, it is now time to crack on with my new hobby—hobby number 2: sausage making. Whilst I was out on my rounds collecting all the Christmas food, I spoke to the butcher about sausages. He reliably informed me that "There's mooooore to sausage making than making sausageeees." And I can tell you, he's not wrong. It's all about percentages; it's math. You can't get the dry versus the wet versus the meat versus the fat wrong. As luck would have it, my math is relatively sharp, so I already have the ratios sorted. The butcher also handed me a couple of meters of casings and his own rusk! I'm halfway there! This lot with my already purchased sausage machine means that I now have everything required to make a perfect Christmas banger!

I have everything laid out in the kitchen. I've converted the millilitres into grams for the digital scales and worked out the ratios of dry to wet. You can't put fresh produce, such as apples, into a sausage as it will rot if you don't eat it immediately or don't freeze immediately and store properly. Hence, you need dried fruits. I have dried cranberries for this, and I am also drying out sprouts in the oven, which I have chopped, shredded, and left on a low heat. They've been on for about two hours and will need another two. And it stinks. It smells like an old people's home and not a nice one, not like Derek. There's a bundle of other ingredients, but a sausage maker never reveals his recipes or ratios, I think. Once everything is ratio ready, I combine it then shove it in and start to pump it through the machine. This then sends my mix into the casings, making sausages! Fucking 'ave it. Lazlo has entered my factory, and he sees what's happening and wants to have a go. He wants to try turning the handle that pumps the meat into the casings. Not a fucking chance.

"Me turn, Daddy."

"No."

"Yes. Me turn."

"No, go away."

"Daddy, me turn, please."

"No, you'll do it too fast, and it'll all end in tears."

"No, I do it nice," he says.

"Aaaargh, okay, just a quick go, and do it slow. Turn the handle nice and slowly," I tell him.

I've lifted him up so he's sitting on the kitchen worktop in a chair called a bumbo or something. He grabs at the handle with a huge smile on his face. He turns the handle...

"Nice and slow, that's really good. Well done," I say to him. This is going well.

And then he whips it around and goes nuts with it, and there's fucking sausage meat everywhere.

Hhhhmm...thinking back, this is just like the hose incident, this is. He promised not to squirt the water anywhere other than the paddling pool, and what did he do after about five seconds of holding it? He got his mum right in the face.

"Lazlo, STOP!" I yell at him. I grab him and put him back down on to the floor, the lower level of the house where he should remain. He just walks off, seemingly happy with his efforts. He couldn't give a single shit about the mayhem he's just caused and the mess he's left behind. Little $%#&*@. I decide to crack open my first beer of the day and then I clean it all up and then I get on with the production line. Once I am done, I plate the meters of sausages that I have created and stick them in the fridge. There's a party to go to tonight, so I want to get ready for that. We spent the night with family and friends, as you do at this time of year. We didn't get home till the early hours. I was pretty smashed, and as I had to get up at 5:30 AM to get the train into the office, it was straight to bed for me. Well, it was straight to bed for all of us in fact.

The next morning, when I come downstairs to grab a coffee before I leave for work, I realize it stinks. My hangover (still a bit drunk) means that the smell is making me want to vom; it's awful. It appears I had forgotten to cover up the sprout-riddled sausages that I had placed in the fridge. I had just popped them in there on a plate with a view of covering them up before freezing them, which I also did not do. If it smells this bad outside the fridge…? I open the door. Fuck me, it's bad. I immediately gag. I get the sausages out, cover them up in cling film, and then put them back. If they can't release any smells, then the fridge will get rid of the smelly vapor that's in there. I grab some industrial-looking smelly spray from under the sink, give it a whirl around the room, and *bingo*. It's all done. By the time the family all get up, this stench will all have faded away. But to be safe, I'll open a window too.

I get to the station and jump on the train. It's pretty bleak, not that many people going into London this time of year. By the time I get to my desk, Christmas seems a distance memory. I then get a text message:

> Martin, what have you done in the kitchen? It absolutely stinks. There's raw meat left on the counters and God knows what else. There's raw

sausages in the fridge, which are leaking! The fluid, whatever that is, is brimming over the plate you left them on and dripping down onto the shelves and the food that SHOULD be in there. You've left raw meat, in and out of the fridge, uncovered and THEN you've tried to hide the smell by using the spray that we use in hospitals to remove the stench of death.

This is unsanitary and dangerous, how could you be so stupid? We are not staying here. The smell alone is making us all gag. I'm taking the boys to a hotel. And we're not coming home until this is all cleaned up.

When you get a message like that, there's not much you can say. So I don't.

I get back that night loaded to the eyebrows with cleaning equipment. I'm not going to make the same mistake I did with the car. It's freezing cold, but at the same time, it is totally necessary to keep all doors and windows open. Good lord, my wife is right. It is bad and the smell… I get the sausages, drain away all the juices, double wrap them, and throw them in the freezer, not wasting them. I'm tackling the issue at source! I get to work on the fridge next, and when that's done, I leave a paper cup full of coffee beans on the top shelf. I got the beans from a mate who owns a coffee shop. The idea is that they will soak up the stench—thank you, Google. Once that's done, I attack the kitchen worktops and cupboard doors, which are splattered with sausage-making remnants, dining table, mop the floors, a squirt of Febreeze with added lemon and Robert's your mother's brother. Merry Fucking Christmas.

PART 12

IT'S GETTING TOO MUCH

I spent most of my working day today out on the different levels of fire escapes, and then I promoted myself to going out on the roof of the office tower. I've been in a constant mood of sadness. I've been telling myself over and over that enough is enough and that it has to stop, and I am right. This has to stop and it will and soon. They say January is the most depressing month of the year. Maybe that's what I have a case of? That and the one where you get sad if you don't see any sun. I might have that too? I once read about a famous musician who had it, and to resolve the matter, he would fly to the Bahamas for six months, not very practical in my case.

I'm going to meet the lads tonight. I really can't face it, but I can't get out of it; so it's onwards and upwards. I'll slap on a fake smile and be the Bertie they all know and like, or something like that. Wrapping up at work, it's pretty dead at the minute; so I get on my way, out of the office and over to meet the lads. At Bishopsgate, I see there's a boy racer who's stopped in traffic. He's also blocking my walking path. He's clearly not anticipated stopping, so by the time he's realized it, he's now blocking the island so no one can cross. The fool. I look at him, and he looks back. He just looks vacant; there's no reaction. He sits there with his baseball cap and tracksuit on just looking at me. He has no idea what an idiot he is. Why didn't he notice the cars in front stopping, the pedestrian crossing zone, and then fucking well stop before he did?

"Drv!" I call out. I say this, and then immediately stuff my tongue over my bottom teeth and into my bottom lip and then add a "Deeerrrrr."

He drives off, seemingly unaffected. I bet that really showed him. Where did the "Deeeerrrr" come from? I've not done that since I was about twelve years old. Anyway, let's ignore the fact that I now seem to be mentally morphing into a small boy and get to the bar.

There's a good few of us out tonight, and it's a change of venue than the norm—the Gherkin. It's in the center of the City of London, has a great bar that does a great Guinness, and it's nicer than the normal shitholes that we usually drink in. Smudger's missus had a kid just before Christmas, and we've not been able to get together before now; so we're all out to wet the baby's head. We're all tightly packed into the bar drinking and chatting. Just next to us is the hot plate bit, the bit where no one is allowed to stand as that's where they put the food out for the waiting staff to grab for distribution. Now, my friends know me. They know what I am like, and they know that anything I say may very well be a windup; so the smart ones are wary. But not all my friends are smart, and sometimes even the smart ones can let their guard drop…

"He fucking told everyone that I was the Santa Claus at Lakeside," Smudger announces to the group to much laughter. Even Smudger is laughing now, after the initial shock and rage of course.

"How was Blackpool anyway?" he then asks.

"Shocking," I reply. "There was one funny bit actually."

"What?" asks Krypton.

"During the weekend we were playing on those car racing arcade games, the ones where you sit in the actual car."

"Wooow, sounds amazing," Big Face says mockingly.

"No, you div." Another DIV, but no tongue in lip this time. "That's not the funny bit," I say.

"Should hope not," says Smudger.

"Anyways, we've been playing on these arcade games for a couple days and it's something like two wins a piece across the board. So I decide that whoever comes last on the next race loses and will have to do a forfeit."

"Like what?" asks Big Face.

"Buy a grot mag on the journey home from a busy service station," I tell him.

Everyone's face smiles and winces at the same time.

"Who lost?" Big Face asks again.

"Fat Bloke," I tell him. "He lost and got the needle about it, which was even funnier. So anyway, on the way back, we stop at these services, and it's banged-out packed. We all go inside, and I tell Fat Bloke that he has to buy the mag from this twenty-one-year-old attractive blonde girl who's working behind the counter."

"That is cold, brutal," says Smudge.

"Yeah, it's great, I know. And then I tell him that he has to pick the *Over 50s Readers Wives* mag. He goes to pieces at this stage, and I don't think he's going to do it. He's moaning and telling us that it's well out of order blahdeblah. So Paul, the geezer whose Stag it is, tells him to man the fuck up and get on with it as he's ruining the Stag weekend."

"So? What happens?" Big Face asks. He's keen to get the bottom of this story clearly.

"He does it. The girl behind the counter gave him one filthy look, but he gets the mag."

"Why do you think things up like that?" Krypton asks.

"Never mind that. That's not the best bit. We jump back in the car, and Side Plate starts flicking through said specialised mag. It's only got Fat Bloke's sister in it!"

"Wow, whoa, fucking hell," the chorus of the majority replies.

"What she like?" said Smudge.

"Fat," I say.

"I admire her for doing it, earning a few quid," says Smudger's mate Fish.

"Yeah, you would. You probably took the photo. You still doing the porn?" Big Face asks him.

146

"It's not porn. It's art."

"Course it is, Fish," I say. "Help yourself to food, mate." As I say this, everyone knows that the food is not ours, not mine, not for this party of people. Everyone knows this, but Fish…he starts to tuck into the food that's been laid out pending pick up from the waiting staff. There's a lot of finger food spread across about four or five plates, and he's not holding back. Deep fried prawns, chips and dips, chicken satay—he's really going for it. I can't help but laugh, and when he finally stops chomping and asks me what I'm laughing at, I drop the bomb that this is not our food. He then scurries away from our area for a few minutes. After calling me a git, obviously. He's called Fish because he's Indian and has a really long name of which one part of it is Fish. I don't actually know if I have any friends who have a normal name?

"What did Fat Bloke say?" says Krypton, getting us back on track.

"He said, 'She's only forty-three, why is she in the over fifties mag?"

I've known Krypton for a long time. We lost touch for a while, but we've been good friends since we were about nineteen. We worked together in a restaurant when I was at college. Tonight in the bar, with him being here, I feel like I want to open up to him, I wish I could open up to him. But that's not going to happen. There're other people here, and there's no way I could even get the words out.

Krypton is the friend whose dad's pond I set on fire. By accident, of sorts. One drunken night we'd managed to cover the pond in debris after getting stupid and chucking crap everywhere whilst being out in his garden. I then had the groundbreaking idea of setting the debris, which was sitting atop of the water, on fire to clear it. The thinking behind the idea was that it would burn the top of the pond only as well as the crap we threw on it. Then as it's on water, the fire would die out. So we sprayed the top of it with petrol and set it alight. Not the best idea, granted. When the fire did eventually go out, the pond was a right fucking mess. It looked like a thousand rainbows had landed on the top of it and had managed to bring a load of dead koi carp with it. When the fish started floating up, we'd realized that we'd royally fucked up. So we then decided the best thing to do was to leave it well alone and look again in the morning. Luckily, Krypton's dad was on holiday at the time, so we had a few days to think something up. In the end, we removed the dead fish and that was about it. Masterminds.

As a young adult, I managed to cause quite a lot of mayhem with Krypton; and even when I hadn't, Krypton, later on in life, told me that he'd blamed me for other shit that had happened when he was questioned by his parents. This actually made perfect sense by that time of telling me, as I did recall there were moments when his parents were a bit frosty towards me. But hey ho, all's well that ends well. The Kryptons are a mad bunch but a genuine bunch, and after all the carnage that I may or may not have caused over the years, I do genuinely love that family.

"What time are you getting to the hotel tomorrow?" Big Face asks me.

"About 10:30."

"Okay, I'll see you then."

"Ooooooohh. You two lovebirds having a secret escape?" says Smudger.

"Idiot, we are going to the darts," I tell him.

"Why didn't you invite me"? Smudger says a little annoyed.

"I didn't wanna," I tell him.

"That's harsh," says Krypton.

"Well, what should I do? Make something up to not hurt his feelings?"

"Yes, that's exactly what you should do," Krypton informs me.

"All right, calm down. Smudge, I wanted to, but I couldn't get any more tickets."

"Piss off, Bertie," says Smudger.

"Ha ha." I laugh. "Okay, my round for being an arsehole?" Everyone seems to nod in agreement.

I know that I'm going to cry tonight, and when I leave the bar and head towards Liverpool Street, the tears come. They last up until I fall asleep on the train. I get back to my local station, and I jump in a cab to get me the rest of the way home from there. The driver's a loon though. He's doing eighty miles per hour on the country lanes, and I'm starting to shit my pants. Three seconds and six miles after getting in the car—well, that's what it feels like—I tell him to pull over. I'm going to walk the rest.

"Twenty quid, mate."

"I'm not giving you a score for that. You drive like a psycho," I tell him.

"What? I've got you back safe. You owe me twenty quid."

"Mate, I owe you jack shit. You're lucky I don't report you. Here's a tenner, and that's all you're getting."

"Well, I'll lock the car."

"Lock it then. I don't give a shit."

"You're not the police. What gives you the right to make judgment?" he says.

"How do you know who or what I am?"

There's a long pause. I think he thinks I could be police.

"Get out then," he demands of me.

I get out and give him his tenner. I'm not near my house as I don't want him to know where I live, so I start to walk. He turns the car around and drives back passed me. He winds down the window and shouts out at me. He calls me a "Dick Head"? Nice. There's an insult there from 1987.

A few weeks ago I got an e-mail whilst at work informing me that the Sunshine Inn Hotel, which I had booked for me and my wife, was now closing on said night due to under occupancy. And so did my friends. They, my friends, then all e-mailed me telling the news about the hotel. This was a problem. You see, I had planned for all of us—wives and girlfriends too—to attend the PDC World Championships. And we were all booked in a hotel within walking distance. I called the hotel and told them they can't close as the PDC is on up the road, but they said they are closing as only nine people

PART 12

are staying. "Yes," I said, "that's my nine!" They just apologized for any inconvenience caused? So I then called the PDC.

"Professional Darts Corporation," the lady answered. I told her of the disaster that's happened and that the hotel is closing on the day and that they'll lose thousands in revenue if the hotel can't accommodate the hundreds of guests that would be staying there in January for the World Championships. And only then did I take a breath. She seemed shocked and upset for me and my dilemma. She then gave me the number of a bloke who books the rooms for her for when the players travel. I called him. I told him of the disaster too. He asked for my name; and when I said Martin Alberts, he said, "Aah yes, you're Heath's mate."

Heath? I'm thinking.

"Heath Keller, are you Heath Keller's mate?"

"Yes! Yes, I am," I tell him. I tell him that I am the friend of the one-time and youngest world champion Heath (things can only get) Keller.

He tells me, "Great, I can give you the player's rates at this hotel near the venue. Just tell me how many rooms you need." So I tell him I need five rooms, four doubles and a single. And *boom*, we're all booked up. The Sunshine Inn can kiss my bald arse.

We drop the boys off with the in-laws the next morning, and I can see the confusion in their faces as I explain why I am taking their angelic daughter to the Darts! "You can drink there, sing, dress up, watch darts, and gamble. There's no need to ever leave. It's everything you need and want," I tell them. I get it. It's not their scene, but it is mine. Ooh it's very much my scene and the scene of my mates. This is one of the rarer occasions where my mates and our other halves all get together. And I can't wait to get there!

"Bertie, slow down," my wife says as we ping along the M25.

"I wanna get there on time, babe. Big Face is meeting us at the hotel for ten-thirty. I don't want to be late. This is going to be great!"

"Okay, just calm down a little bit. We're not going to be late."

150

"This is going to be brilliant. Everyone's well up for today. Be good to see some old faces and meet their ladies. I've not seen Worzel for ages."

"Why is he called Worzel?"

"Cause when he was a kid, he was in a fancy dress competition as Worzel Gummidge."

"Did he win?"

"Second. Toya Wilcox won."

"What did you go as?"

"I didn't go as anything. I never knew him then."

"So why…never mind." She trails off with a shake of the head.

When we arrive at the hotel, I see that Big Face has just parked up. So we head into the reception together and get the keys for our rooms. Big Face and I both chuck the bags in the correct rooms, and then we head to the bar and wait for the others to arrive. Our wives stay in the rooms to get changed. Don't know why they didn't come ready. We both did? After twenty minutes or so, we are all here and the girls are now all changed. There're two types of conversation, and both are going on in the bar at the same time as people greet each other: there's ours, the men, and then there's theirs, the ladies.

"All right, Bigface, you bellend." Men.

"Hi, Jo, how have you been? Are your parents okay?" Women.

"Shit, Krypton, who dressed you today?" Men.

"Oh wow, you look lovely. Did you have a nice Christmas?" Women.

"I'm hanging out my arse here. Got shit-faced last night at Fuego's after you left." Men.

"Your hair looks amazing." Women.

"Was Dirty Pete working there?" Men.

"And you've lost weight." Women.

"Right, fat boys, we all here? Let's get some taxis over to the venue for some arrears!" Men.

When our taxis pull up onto the rough-arse gravel outside the PDC World Darts Championship arena, I leap out like a cat. I'm first to get into the building, and I find our table that's been reserved. A very long and narrow table is set for all of us to comfortably fit along. There's a long sheet of absorbent paper covering it. It's to soak up the spilled beer, I guess. The ladies take their seats, and the men head off to hunt and gather. Then the music kicks in, and I'm buzzing "Da da da da daaaa da da da da daaaa da da da da daaaa OI OI OI." Helpful and Worzel have headed over to the bar to get the beer. Krypton, Big Face, and I are over at the bookies putting some bets on. The bookies are rammed; there's at least six people in each queue waiting to get the counter. We're three of the six in our line. Big Face starts moaning about me climbing on him, but I can't stop. I'm too excited! We're all putting stupid bets on that will never realistically win. For example, we all bet that there will be a nine-darter, which is ridiculously rare. But we don't really care, it's about taking part. Whilst standing at the counter handing over my money to Beverly, who looks about as happy to see me as a dog does a vet, I notice one of the players in the other queue. I don't really know him, but he's dressed like a dart player; so I flick through my program, and I recognize his picture from the players who are listed in it. I decide to go over to him and get him to sign my program, on the page that has his picture on it.

"Who's that?" Krypton asks me upon my return to the queue.

"Ermm…Richie Green."

"Who's Richie Green?"

"He's that bloke there." I point to him.

"No, you wally. Why is he signing your program?"

"He's a dart player. I'm thinking of getting more signatures."

"That's a great idea. We should fill the program up with all the players' signatures, the ones that we can find."

"Let's do it!" I say. The gauntlet has been thrown down, and I fully intend to get them all.

Worzel then comes over to where we are. "I've just got some drinks for the ladies, and Helpful is getting some jugs in for the table," he tells us.

"We're getting signatures from the players in our programmes. Well, me and Krypton are. I've just snagged Richie Green."

"I'm going to go and buy some darts," says Worzel.

"Great idea, I'll come with you."

Worzel and I head off and tell the others we'll meet back at the table. There's not really a shop. It's more of a long counter that's filled with all dart paraphernalia. It looks like the same type of counter you see when you enter a cinema, just without the popcorn machine. There're bundles of stuff though: shirts, beer mats, hats, whistles, dartboards, pint glasses—loads and loads of great stuff.

I buy myself two sets of darts with extra flights and a Union Jack fake leather carry case, very classy. I put them in my back pocket and leave them hanging out a bit at the top. People might see them and think I'm a player!

Whilst I'm at the shop, pretending to be a player, I spot another dart player, a Japanese one! That's gotta be a rare signature. Should be worth more than a normal English one in the grander scheme of things. When I get back to the table, the first thing I do is ask Krypton how many he's got. He's up to three already? Apparently, they just keep walking past our table. I flash him a look at my program. He sees the scribble.

"I see your three, and I raise you a Sheygo Apasada! Japanese." I nod smugly.

"That's a great one," Krypton says admirably.

"I just got a Dutch one, Vincent van den Barnfelt. Got him to sign my darts case," says Worzel.

"Did he have enough room?" I ask.

"Just."

The ladies are all chatting away, and although I think they might have been a tad sceptical about a day at the darts, they're really getting into the atmosphere; it's just fun here, nothing else, just fun. The first match is about to start, and the players are ready to enter the stage. It's like a boxing walk on! They have music, smoke machines, and an entourage of security. And the best bit is, they're right next to us! We are sat bang next to the aisle of the walk-ons. An added bonus I did not expect.

"I'm going to get on the TV," my wife states. This makes sense to us all. We all want to get on TV. So when the MC gets up on stage and starts announcing the player who's standing next to us, we immediately start to look very excited and begin clapping and cheering. The cameraman though is a blatant sexist and is only interested in filming the women, fucker. Drastic times call for drastic measures. So when the player, who's signature I have also obtained, starts his walk on, I lean over the barrier and in front of him, almost a bit too much, but I do get on TV. After a few of the matches I've realized that looking excited can get you on TV but looking nervous and stressed works even better. We all then take the approach of showing our best concerned looks when the cameras are near, and between us, we must make up about 85 percent of the viewed audience. So much so that I got a text from Smudger that read. "Get the fuck off my TV."

I charged all around the venue getting signatures from as many people as I could find that morning and early afternoon. Right up to 2:00 PM. That's when the morning session finished and we, sadly, had to head back to the hotel. We have a meal in the bar and then get changed. We're not going back to the darts for the evening session, but it would be nice to change into evening wear I feel. At about six o'clock we're all in full flow. The evening session is on the TV, and my Japanese mate is playing! We're also playing darts whilst in the hotel bar, and we're playing halve its, not 501. It is then that Big Face comes over to me and whispers in my ear, "Go to reception now." I look back confused and a tad wary. "Go, go now." Hhhmm okay, I'll go and see what is it he wants me to see, but warily.

As I get there, I look about, and stone me, it's only the PDC world champion Pete the Tower standing at check-in! Nice, I get him to sign my program and then strut back into the bar.

"Got any new signatures?" I ask Krypton.

"Nope, my program is back in the room." *Boom!* I open the page with The Tower's signature on it and shove it in his face. "Jesus

Schweps. Where did you… Is he staying here?" he shouts out with a look of excited realization.

"Yep—just checked in."

"Well played, sir, well played."

"Thanks."

An hour or so later and the bar is full of dart players. They're all playing tomorrow and have checked into the hotel tonight. This is great. I get all the signatures apart from one miserable git who refuses to sign anyone's program. He just looks back all stone-faced to anyone who asks—twat. During one of our games of halve its, my wife needed a bull's-eye to win, so she nonchalantly turns to The Tower and asks The Tower if he wouldn't mind getting her a bull's-eye! He gladly obliges, nice man. However, during our next game, a stranger asks us if he could use the dartboard. Can he not see that we are? I tell him he can but just as soon as we're finished, but he's a bit insistent. He really wants to use the dartboard. I tell him to hang on, we're nearly done and that we were here first, so he'll have to wait. He says he wants to practice, but I tell him I don't care and we'll be ten minutes, maybe longer, and he can wait. Some people, they're just rude. That man turned out to be Darren Gurnley, who happened to be playing that night, but I didn't know that at the time. I only found out two hours later when I looked up and he was on the TV.

PART 13

SPICE TIME

"Your taxi is here," my wife calls out to me.

"All right, hang on a sec, I'm just clearing up the wallpaper Lazlo has ripped off the wall," I call back. Cost me twenty-six quid a roll that did. The little git. I walk back into the lounge where my wife and the little angels are sitting on the sofa watching a film.

"Okay, I'll see you then. I'll call you tomorrow, and I'll bring something nice back," I tell them all. My wife is upset because I happen to be going to India for a week with work. I don't even want to go. I'll be all alone. I fucking hate being on my Jack. I am actually going to meet some vendors when I get there, but I can't imagine that being fun. Alas, the "dream" or the thought of what a business trip is like is far and away removed from the actual. Still, being on my own in a dusty country five thousand miles away from anyone I like, love, or mildly care about would appear to be some people's ideal dream, not mine. I don't want to go. I never do. Being away from everyone, I have found, is a trigger for the Wobbles. Let's just hope I don't burst into tears with the taxi driver.

"So...I'll be off then," I say with an apologetic tone. "I'll be back Friday. It's only Monday to Thursday that you'll not see me. It will go quick."

"Okay fine, see you later," she says.

Hhmm, I don't think it is fine. It doesn't fucking well feel fine. I give the kids a hug, and then I uncling Lazlo from my neck. God, I hope he behaves. Then I leave the frost of the family home and enter the deadness life of corporate travel. This is going to suck. So let's just get it done and dusted.

"Heathrow, right?"
"Yep," I tell the driver.
"Terminal?"
"Five, please."
"Oh yeah, BA."
"Yeah, BA," I tell him.
"I flew BA once before, nightmare," He just kept saying.
"Ain't getting on no plane, sucka." I look over at the driver, smiling.
"Oh…oh, okay," he says, looking confused. That's gold that, how does he not crack a smile? Never mind, looks like this'll be a long drive. Heathrow is a nightmare at the best of times. The traffic around the airport starts from about ten miles away, so even if you get there on time, you're still another hour fighting to get into the damn building. We navigate all that, and I get to the airport in good enough time. I always have to be at an airport, at the very least, three hours before I fly. I always feel very anxious right up to the point of check-in. Right up until I see my bags go off up the black rubber runway to the place where they get sat on, thrown around, run over, and drowned in muddy water by the caring baggage handlers. Up until that point, I am always a fucking wreck. Still, that bit's now done. Right, off to the lounge, I may as well get a few beers in me before I take off to pastures unknown. I have zero expectations and zero knowledge of where it is I am heading off to, so I may as well face it with a beer in hand.

These lounges can be total madness at times. It's as if people haven't eaten for months and need to cram in as much free food as humanly possible for the time that they are there. I grab crisps and nuts, that's all—oh, and the beer. I grab a good few Tiger beers from the fridge, nab a paper, and take a seat on the sofa. I don't want to be up and down every five minutes, so I stock up and stake a claim on what is now my location. I can't relax though. I am thinking about everything and anything, going over and over all fucked-up scenarios in my head. There are things I should be doing and things I need to get done. I can't do any at the moment as I am sitting in an airport. How am I going to get all these little jobs that I need doing done from here? Best get a few beers down me. I'm probably just tired, and a few beers will help me relax so that I can sleep on the plane. I look around, and I notice there's a woman looking at me with an odd stare. I then notice why she is doing so. I appear to be talking to myself, talking aloud. The panic and worry flying around my head is now being heard by others as I mutter and moan at an audible level. That's a new symptom. Normally it's in the head and stays in the head only. Now I mutter-rant at strangers who just so happen to be nearby. I grab my phone and call my brother. I want to be reassured. Not sure what I want to be reassured about, but I could just do with a friendly voice. This is bad. I've only been away from home for a few hours, and this has come on. And it has come quick.

"Hello."

"Hey, mate, you all right?"

"Yeah, good, thanks. Just got back from the park. About to order myself a fifteen-quid kebab."

"Fifteen quid? For a kebab?"

"Yeah, it's massive. I'll send you a picture. It comes with doner meat, chicken, sheesh meat, lamb, chips salad, and the pita is the size of a large naan bread."

"Ain't sheesh meat and lamb the same thing?"

"Dunno, might be. This is fully loaded and they stick a bundle of chilies on it too."

"Sounds nice."

"You okay, mate? Where are you?"

"At the airport."

"Aah yeah, you off to India today, right?"

"I am."

"Are you larging it in the business lounge?"

"I am."

"Lucky git, they don't let me in those types of places."

"What do you mean?"

"Well...I'm a builder, ain't I? Those places are all full of suits and briefcases."

"I'm not wearing a suit, and I don't have a briefcase."

"You know what I mean."

"Not really."

"So is all the beer and food free?"

"Well, it comes in with the price of the ticket, so not really."

"Which you didn't pay for."

"If you look at it that way, then the entire trip is free."

"Nice, I could do with some of that. Apart from all the free stuff, everything okay?"

"Yeah, it's just that...you know, I'm just on my own."

"Aaah, I see. Well, try not to panic. Do you need a business partner?" he asks me.

"Yeah, I do, in fact. Why? Do you know someone?"

We both laugh at that. But he knows and he knows what to do and say. Either he's a psychological genius or he just knows what to say and when to say it to his little brother.

"You'll be fine, mate. Have a couple of beers, get on the plane. They'll probably have champagne, won't they? Watch a film or two, rest up. My phone is always on, so just buzz it anytime you want. I got your back, bro."

"Ah, cheers, mate. I'm gonna need you this week."

"I'm going nowhere. Think of all the great curry you're going to eat."

"Ha yeah, cheers, mate. Right, order your kebab. I'll call you in a day or so."

He signs off with "Enjoy the land of the rising sun." Geography is not his strong point.

"Okay? See ya, mate. Thanks a lot."

After I board and get settled in my booth, I am quickly approached by a young lad who has been walking up and down the aisle offering drinks on a skinny silver tray.

"Would you like a drink, sir?"

"Oooh is that white wine?" I ask him as I point at the tray.

"It's champagne, sir."

"You can take the kid out of southeast London…" I say.

"Sorry, sir?"

"Champagne is fine, mate. I'll take two." My brother was right. I'll tell him when I land.

"Newspaper, sir?"

"Yes, please."

"I only have *Daily Mails* left, is that okay?"

"Nah, you're alright, mate. I'm good for stories about Lady Diana, Hitler, Churchill, and Thatcher."

"Okay, sir. Please just call if you need anything. Can I suggest you preview the food menu as we will be taking orders shortly after takeoff?"

"Okay, mate, will do. Thanks."

After dinner I get stuck into the new Rocky Balboa film. I'm also about ten beers and three champagnes into the journey at this stage. There's an emotional part to the movie. Rocky gets ill. He's my hero. I have pictures of Balboa up all around my house. He can't die, no fucking way. I need to get a breather, so I pause the film and head to the bar where I meet a stewardess.

"Are you okay, sir?" She can see that I am visually upset.

"I am, I am…I'm upset actually. Have you seen the new Rocky film?"

"I have, yes," she tells me.

"Well, he's sick, and he's my absolute hero. I'm devastated here. I had to stop the film and come here to the bar so that I can compute all that's happening. He can't die on me."

She looks back at me with some concern and nods the nod. The nod that says, "Don't worry, I'm sure it'll be fine." Or is it the nod that says, "Get ready for more shit, mate, cause it's going to get rough?" I decide to take a quick shot of tequila and then get back to the film. Rocky has always made me act in a certain way—laugh or cheer, jump up and start fighting my brother—but never has it brought me to tears before. My emotions seem to be pretty erratic.

After landing, I get picked up by the hotel car and am taken to where I shall stay until Friday morning. It's six in the morning, and I am still fully on drinking time; so whilst at reception, I utilize the twenty-four-hour bar. I say bar; it's a big fridge where you can help yourself and bill it to the room. I am not at all tired, and also, as it's now Monday, I will need to head to the offices. Well, one of them. We have three potential places, and I want to get them all done today and tomorrow. After going to these local offices, I also want to speak to other firms that are set up out here, and only then, I can fly back. I consume a couple of cold bottled beers, and then I head to my room. I should get some sleep now for a couple of hours and then head to work. The working day here starts on average at around 2:00 PM, so I have time to grab a shower and rest.

After waking up, I survey the immediate surroundings. The room is very nice actually. The whole hotel is. The hotel is on a private road, and my room overlooks the private gardens and pool. But the second you look outside of the hotel grounds, out over the back of the gardens, or step onto the street, the first thing you notice is the total chaos. Are we really looking to set up shop here? I mean, I haven't been into the offices yet, but by the looks of things here in Hi-Tech City, I'm not so sure it's exactly advanced or Hi-Tech for that matter. Still, let's have a look and see what all the fuss is about. Why are so many other firms coming out here?

Down at reception I tell them I need a car to take me to the first office that I wish to see and that I may need to go to another after that. They tell me not to worry and that they will provide me with a driver and that he will be with me all day. So he's just going to sit and wait for me all day. Really? It turns out yes, really, he is now mine, and he will be at my beck and call for the next twenty-four hours. I walk out of the hotel and see my driver who appears to be fucking elated about the fact that he's mine for the day. He's got the biggest smile slapped on his face as he comes over to meet me. He's about four feet tall, has a limp, and he now has to drive me around in this mayhem all day. What's he got to be so happy about? We head off toward the office, and just as we leave the hotel's private road, we get stuck alongside a heard of buffalo. The driver seems a bit care-free with regard to them. He's almost running them over. He's very close, and he keeps banging the horn. I don't think that the buffalo realize the rules of the road. The car horns are all that I can hear. It's a constant loud buzzing hum that pollutes the air and never seems to stop. We're only five minutes from the office, but it takes about twenty-five minutes to get there as we never get over fifteen miles per hour. Although at any opportunity the driver sees available, he totally floors it. I'm in a constant violent rocking motion all the way there. When I get out, the driver gives me his card and tells me to call when I am ready to leave and he will be outside waiting. "But please, sir, can you give me ten minutes notice?" Seems fair enough.

So here I am. I'm at work. I made it in, and now I have to walk around looking impressed. I have to meet a few people and really try to see what this place is like with the people in mind mainly. I can do that. I'm quite good at putting on a false face, so this should be a fucking breeze. It takes me about ten minutes to get into the building as I have to write down my life story into a book that is kept by the security team that sit outside the actual entrance. They also spot that I have a laptop, so I have to write down the serial code, model, year it was made, and colour. It feels like it's about thirty degrees, which it probably is, so I want to get inside as soon as I can; and this hold up is getting on my nerves. I make it past them and go through a turn-stile where I am met by a senior manager from the vendor that we are looking to invest in. He's all smiles and takes me up to the third floor where I then have to report everything I did downstairs again, but in a new book! The security here seem to think that I am happy with what they are doing? They appear to think that I approve of their professional and thorough processing of me. I don't, but they seem happy enough. After the meeting and the sales pitch, I decide that I want to meet some of the people and to look around the site. I don't really want a chaperone, but I have managed to collect a full-blown entourage. I do try to speak to the teams and the individual team members; but every question I ask is answered by the management with management spiel, so it's a wasted effort.

We go for a coffee in the canteen. I am handed a small metal cup that's full to the brim with very sweet and very hot coffee that has already had milk and sugar added for my benefit. The cup is hotter that the sun itself and to be able to physically hold it you would need hands made of asbestos. I quickly put it down on the table next to me where a group has just finished lunch. I know that they have finished because there's rice absolutely fucking everywhere. I look back to the coffee guy, and just as he is about to hand back the change to my potential colleague, we, the coffee man and I, spot a cockroach run across the counter. In an unsaid, unspoken knowing silence we both decide to ignore the roach. I didn't drink the coffee. Instead I said to my entourage that I would really appreciate it if I could speak to a team alone just to gauge their communication skills and that it is probably best if the entourage are not around as it might add extra pressure to the team. They seem nervous as it is. They agree and set up a meeting in the "Free Time Zone." Said zone has a coffee machine, table football, and bean bags! I've not had a meeting on a beanbag before; well, not one that I wasn't stoned in. As I wait the five minutes I was told it would be till the teams turn up, I grab a coffee from the vending machine and read through the *Hindustan Times*. I find a story about a guy who was locked out of his house late one night. He decided to scale the outside of the building up to the sixth floor where he planned to break in through the balcony. He died after falling fifty feet into oncoming traffic.

The five minutes I wait turns into ten then fifteen, which annoys me quite a lot. And during this time someone comes in and sticks up a sign on the coffee machine that says, "Do Not Use Worms." Sadly I have to ask the boiler suit-wearing, sign-hanging man what the fuck that means.

"What does that mean?"

"Yes, sir, do not use."

"Why?"

"Yes, sir. No use. Worms, sir."

"Worms in coffee? How the fuck do you get worms in coffee?"

He nods, smiles again, says "Yes, sir" once more, and leaves. Nice! My potential employee then comes in with a gleaming smile and says hello. Not "Sorry for the delay" or any explanation for that matter as to why it took fifteen minutes to walk twenty feet from her desk.

"Some geezer has just come in here and put that sign on the coffee machine," I tell her whilst pointing at the machine.

"Yes, you shouldn't drink this."

"What do they mean by worms?"

"Oh, they get sometimes small worms, the white little ones in the coffee beans."

"Do you mean maggots?"

"Maggots?" She looks confused.

I google a picture, and she agrees with the image and that worms are in fact maggots. And I've just had an espresso's worth. I speak to a few employees that day, all of whom seem terrified to speak to me and all of whom are late. I start to understand that time is not an important thing here; in fact, it is secondary to pretty much everything. IST is a time zone that exists here, and there's not much chance of that changing. So if we move here, Indian Stretchable Time is something we will have to accept.

Outside the building the happiest limp-infected driver is again fucking elated to see me. As I am leaving the building and I sign the books to confirm I am now leaving, I notice him standing to attention at his car with the biggest smile slapped across his chops. He seems very pleased that I am his shipment, and as I approach, he calls out to a few other drivers who are nearby and gives them a knowing show-off type of a wink and head wobble. What is the head wobble? It doesn't mean yes and it doesn't mean no? I'll ask about that later.

"I need to go to Sheelparaman Market, please." I try to announce it correctly. A guy at the office said I should go and have a look but not to go alone and not to go in the middle of the day as it's too hot. Well, it's not the middle of the day, so...

"Chilparaman?" the driver asks.

"Sheelparaman," I reply.

"Sheeeel-pa-ra-man?" He comes back with slowly.

"Yes, the market. You know the market?" I should have learned some Hindi. I hate not knowing any words in a country I am in. I can get you two beers in pretty much all of Europe and parts of Asia.

"No, sir."

"Hmm, okay, hang on." I go back in the building. I am going to find the guy who told me to go there. He can explain to the driver where to go. Trouble is, the security now want me to fill out all the details again, and I don't want to do that. So I hurdle the turnstile and jump in the lift. As the doors on the lift are closing, all I can hear is "No, sir. No, sir. Please no, sir." Too late now though, I have fully committed to being a rogue entrant into the building. It's now a matter of time. I need to find the guy and get him to come to the car and explain where I want to go. It better be worth it. The lift goes up, and I dash out onto the landing area where the teams sit. I can't get into the floor as I don't have a pass and it's a secure area. Not to worry, I just ask the security guy who was sitting there to let me in, and he does just that! I'm in, and now I need to find... I look in my notes. Kartik, I'm looking for Kartik. I ask someone if they know where Kartik sits, but I all I get back is a blank look. I start to yell out across the floor, "Kaaarrtiiik, Kaaaarrtiiik, it's me, Martin. Where do you sit?" It works. Kartik jumps up. Well, about six people do, but I spot the Kartik I need and head over to him.

"Hey, mate, I need you a minute. Can you come out to my car, please?"

On the way out of the building, I explain to Kartik the situation, and he is only happy to help. As the lift doors open back on the ground floor, there's a load of security all milling around and looking worried. The relief in their faces is clear as they all start to smile upon my arrival back on the outskirts of the building. The security then start to speak to Kartik, and he looks nervous; but I tell them to leave him alone as I need him. I ask Kartik to come with me. I pull him through the crowd and over to the driver who is now back standing to attention and grinning.

"Kartik, can you tell him please to take me to the market you mentioned?"

"Shilparamam," he then says.

"Okay, sir," says the driver.

"Is that it? That's what I said to you," I tell the driver.

"Err, the security says you need to sign the book," Kartik tells me, looking confused.

"Never mind that, mate, I have to go. Thanks very much." I shake his hand, and he runs back into the building. Me and the driver then hit the not-so-open road and head towards the market. It better be good after all this shit.

On arrival I am told that I need to pay to get in. New one on me. And I need to pay foreigner charges too! It's cheaper to go in if you're local. But it's only about sixty pence, so I'm good for it. Wow, what a place. They should charge double to get in here. Well, more than double. I'd well pay more to get in. This place is amazing, and I appear to be quite popular too. You can buy all sorts of great things here, and the market itself seems to be alive. It's buzzing with colour and smells of spice and food being cooked. You can buy artwork, kitchen tools, dresses, saris, table runners, pots, pans, pashminas, rugs, chairs, toys, jewelry. There's one guy selling live chickens! I can live here. This is a great experience. I could definitely live here. I fucking love this. Right, I need to shop, haggle, and get some gifts for the wife and the boys. I need to find something that Lazlo can't break easily is my first challenge. None of that "Made in China" crap. That shit never lasts in my house. I see a guy selling kites. He can't smash that up if it's in the air, can he?

"How much are the kites?"

"Two hundred," he says.

"Fifty," I go back with.

"150," he says.

"Fifty," I say. He looks at me oddly. He is of the impression that I will move on the price; I will not. It's not that I don't want to get ripped off. I like the challenge. I also need to know how low I can go on further purchases percentage wise before the deal is off the table. And I am pretty sure that there will be other kite sellers.

"Not fifty. I can't sell for fifty. I will lose money."

"All right, mate. Don't sell it then."

I walk off and start to look at another stall that has wooden elephants sculpted inside other wooden elephants. After a minute, Kite Man approaches me and says okay to the fifty deal. Great news. So I give him fifty rupees, and he gives me three kites! I thought I was haggling for one, not 3, felt a bit bad after that. Not for long though. I get an absolute bundle of goods from all sorts of stalls and sellers, and I don't break twenty quid. There was only one person I managed to piss off actually. It was a lady who got so hacked off she snatched back her items and waved me off. All the others took the 75 percent discount I was offering. Then, just as I was leaving the market, this one guy approaches me and offers to buy my shoes.

"Hey, nice shoes. I will buy them."

"My shoes?"

"Yes, I can have your shoes."

"You want my shoes? What size are you?"

"Yes, size. I am your size."

"If I sell my shoes to you, what am I going to wear?"

"I can sell you some shoes," he tells me.

I have to laugh. I decline his offer, thank him for liking my shoes, and head back to Mr. Happy the Driver.

Next morning I have to meet with more and more people—more forms, more ill-required bag checks and rules, and most of all, more food. Jesus fuck me sideways can these guys consume. I learn to eat with my hand—not like chips, chips are easy—these guys can eat rice with their hands! It's a sort of cup, scoop, and shovel into the gob technique. Goes fucking everywhere, but people seem not too bothered about the mess. People have very singular jobs. Someone will wipe up rice, another will wipe up water, but not both... Oh no, that's not my job, that's the water boy's job. I'm the rice boy! It's a crazy experience; I quite like it, most of it. I didn't like not sleeping for four days as I sat awake in the hotel room thinking about all the jobs and little things that would be requiring my hand the moment I get back. The list grew; it grew by the hour… It's hard. Hard to stop. This list is growing. So is the tension. So is the manic outbursts. So is the crying. Everything is just growing and getting bigger and more out of control. Still, it is what it is. Onwards and upwards, Bertie, it'll be okay soon, I'm sure. The rest of the week is a blur of meetings and dashes to the toilet. If anyone offers you draft beer in India, don't accept it would be my advice. On some days I thought I was going to full on empty.

PART 14

IS THIS IT?

It's my birthday tomorrow. I'll no longer be thirty-three. I'll still be me though. I'll still be crying in the streets, locking myself in toilets for fifteen-minute daily breakdowns, walking around empty office floors and thinking about driving into ditches. And I'll still be an arsehole. There's no getting away from that.

This morning I left for London, but before I left the house, I kissed the boys and took the letters out from their hiding place. I left them out, not in plain sight but also not quite so hidden as they once were. They'll be found in time, and then all the things that need to be taken care of can be. I feel relieved knowing that everything will be taken care of. Everyone will be relieved. This is fine.

The train feels different today. It's warm, and if I could, I would never get off. It trundles through the first few stations, and I see the faces of the people who have been with me through this journey for the last few months. They're not friends, but they're not strangers either. The four ladies get on the train one stop after I do. They always seem to have a funny story to reveal to each other and some added drama. Today one of them had a story about a leak in the kitchen, and although having a slightly flooded room, the fact that the husband had fallen as he entered the room to fix the leaky tap landing "flat on his arse" gave them all and I much joy. They natter from the moment they get on until they part ways at Liverpool Street station. They seem to be such good friends; they seem to have a caring side that they genuinely show to each other. I don't think that anyone I know would think that way about me.

It's a bright day. "Fresh," some people would say. The sun as it comes through the train's window is warm, but don't be fooled, it's still going to be cold when we all get off and trudge up the platform and out of the station. At Stratford, one stop before I usually get off, I get off. I decide to get off. I want to change today. I don't want it to be the same, so I decide I'll take a bus or a tube or maybe another train the remainder of the way. There's a lot of options for me today. I've left my train pass on the seat of the train that I just got off. Maybe someone will find it and use it. Shame to waste it; it cost thousands. What to do…? I think I'll take a wander around the new shopping center that's at Stratford. I've not been in there yet, might be some good stuff to look at. There's a pedestrian bridge that takes me over the tracks and up to the center; it's pretty big. It reminds me of being about sixteen.

When I was at college, I would wander around a lot in shopping centers. Never on a weekend when it would be busy, I preferred to go early in the day or midafternoon during everyone else's working hours. I would look in some shops, mainly music and video shops. I would look at all the films or CDs that I wanted and would one day get. I would look at the posters too. I used to love to see what new ones were out, and I would stare and stare at the picture and try to think about the film or the person in the picture. If it was a new film that I hadn't seen, I would try to invent the film in my head, and later, I could tell people who hadn't seen it that I had. And then I could tell them about the part that I had made up. The music and films shops now though always seem to have a sale on. They have deal upon deal for bulk-buying films. You can even mix and match music with film! That's a new one. I think I'll buy a remastered Blu-ray version of *First Blood* and a vinyl copy of "Sit Down" by James. Not today, but when I come back or the next time I walk passed.

This place is so wide! You can't tell what the shops are selling across the forecourt because it's so big. This will take me ages to get round.

I don't want to walk around in here anymore and as I'm near the Tube, I'm going to go to the West End. The Central Line is a good tube—nice seats, better than the District Line seats—and from Stratford I can go straight to Oxford Circus. As I come up the stairs from the underground and out on to the street, I am met by the masses of people traveling in all directions, all of whom are getting ready to work for the day. Most look stressed. They look gray, sad, and have one ambition that is to get to the office at all costs. Shove that old lady out of the way, I need to send a spreadsheet out. I am in everyone's way. I'm not moving at pace; I'm trundling in odd directions. This is not acceptable. I hear tuts and "Excuse me" said in a hurried whisper. I don't give a fuck about moving. I even stood on the escalator earlier. That's not the norm. You have to walk. Although the stairs are already moving, you still have to walk. Not today and not me.

When I was about twenty-five, I used to meet some old college friends in the West End, we would meet in the same pub at least once a year. I think I'll find it. With the twenty-four-hour drinking rule now in place in the UK, it might even be open. In fact, I'm almost right outside it. I would be if I had come out of another exit from the station. The Argyll Arms is a Tardis of a pub, small on the outside and big on the inside with lots of rooms and hidden corners. I've always liked it. It looks closed though plus I don't need a drink anyway. Tottenham Court Road is at one end of where I am, and Piccadilly Circus is in the other direction. I think Piccadilly wins, so I head off that way. The West End people versus the City people is something that had always made me think. Why are we so different? I am what is known as a 'City Boy—I'm in a suit and dressed to reflect that. The West Enders dress differently and are not a smoothly running organized group. They don't all walk in the same direction at the same speed. They dash, stroll, jog in all directions. Once when I was in a club here after work, I was encouraged to "lose the suit." But I like the suit; I like different.

There's a lot of homeless out this morning. I must pass at least fifteen as I head toward my next destination. Why would they want to congregate in the same place? Surely the odds of getting hand-outs would be far shorter if they were the only homeless person in the town or village? There's a bus that's going south of the river, so I jump on. Piccadilly will have to wait for whenever. Not been on a London bus for ages. The last time I tried to get one, the fucker drove off. This bus is empty. I sit upstairs and take a homemade tour of London, Covent Garden, St. Paul's Cathedral, and then a sharp right over London Bridge and into Bermondsey where I get off. A walk along the south bank is in order. I know that the Swinging Tit pub will be open, so if needed, I can get a livener in there before heading to the city. I should call my brother. I sit down at a spot on the river opposite the Tower of London and look out across the river and at the tourists who are wandering up and down waiting to get fleeced by all and sundry.

"Hi, mate, it's me."

"Hey, you not working today?" my brother asks.

"I am, just on a break." Lie number 1.

"Everything all right?"

"Yeah, you?" Lie number 2.

"Yeah, good. Just got a job to price up today over in Peckham, so should be a short day. What you after?"

"Nah, nothing, just on a break. So I'll give you a call, shoot the breeze. Have you spoken to our sister lately?"

"Err yeah. She's on holiday, I think."

"Yeah, I thought so. I called but didn't get through. Tell her I called if you speak to her." Lie number 3.

"Okay, I'll pop round at the weekend or tomorrow. We can meet for a beer after work. Got your present in the van."

"Okay, I'm busy tomorrow night, mate, so shall we pencil in the weekend? Be good to see you." Lie number 4.

"Yeah, yeah, the weekend's good."

"Okay, look. Goodbye mate," I tell him.

"Aye?" he sounds confused.

"Goodbye. I have to shoot off, need to get back upstairs." Lie number 5.

"Oh right, yeah. Err, see ya, mate."

I hang up. I feel the tears behind my eyes starting to build up. I didn't want to cry down the phone, so I had to hang up. I feel the phone buzz in my pocket. It's a text buzz, not a call buzz. I don't read it. It's going to say something like *"Is everything okay?"* Everything isn't okay, but it will be soon.

As I head up the south bank and pick a bridge to cross, I can feel the phone buzzing in my pocket. *It's going to run out of battery if it keeps this up* is my first thought. It's nearly eleven o'clock. I should show my face in the office. But first, I think I'll cross over Tower Bridge and then walk through St. Katherine Dock. I can go around Wapping and pop into the Captain Kid pub. They do some weird home brew in there. Maybe I should finally try it. I used to run around this part of Wapping when I was a bit fitter. The cobble roads were absolute killers on my knees. But it was clarity in that time that I look back on. I seem to think that back then everything was clear in my mind, and all was okay as I look back. I know that this is bullshit. When the fuck was anything okay? I remember crying on the bus coming home from school. No one was near me then. No one had upset me, yet I was upset. What were the good times? When we look back on our lives, what were the good times? Did anyone I meet ever have a good time, did they? Did I? Why the fuck am I now standing in Wapping talking aloud to myself?

I have a moment of clear thought. I should destroy all my bank cards. If they are found, some bastard can go on a shopping spree. I'll get some cash, and the cards can be chucked. There's not much in Wapping, to be fair, and after fifteen minutes of walking and looking at the DLR, I stop at a cash machine. I get five hundred quid and head to the DLR. I'll take it over to Tower Hill station and walk into the city from there. Don't know if you've ever tried but buying a ticket for the DLR is almost impossible. I can't find a ticket machine anywhere. As I get on, I see a train worker, who I approach and ask to buy a ticket from. They tell me that they don't sell tickets and that the ticket machine is located outside the station along the road a little way. I offer cash, but they won't take it; and as I'm only going one stop, they allow me to ride for free. This is new!

Tower Hill is a funny place for me; I met my wife here in a sort of way. We had met before, but just not in England. When we did meet in England, I brought her to one of the worst bars in the City—Harvey's at Tower Hill. I also had a fight here once. It was shortly after I'd started work in the City. And lastly but not surprisingly I had a mental breakdown of sorts by the sandwich shop on the corner. Still onwards and upwards, I can't hang around here reminiscing all day. I need to get rid of the cards, so…I was thinking of chucking them in the Thames. But that's now behind me, and I don't want to go back on myself. So a drain maybe? I'm going to look odd kneeling down by a drain emptying my wallet. Maybe I should throw them under a car…nah that's not going to do anything other than get them all dirty. Drain it is. I'll split each card up and then drop one piece in a different drain as I go along. I have three cards. that's now six pieces, and I'll alternate streets and the side of the road to chuck each part of them.

About twenty-five minutes later, I'm now at Bishopsgate with one piece of bank card left. I drop it down the drain right outside the police station and then I look along the road a little to where the Bishopsgate Institute is. I spent many an afternoon in there studying and writing assignments for my degree. As I recall, that was a nice time. I used to like academia. It took me away from the office and made me stand out among others who were doing the day-to-day. I was different. I studied in my lunch hour and before work. I was different. I didn't just have a job, I had a degree to go and get, and get it I would. University wasn't on the cards, not when I was sixteen, but being able to study and get a degree was. Just as long as I could work and study at the same time.

I am going to go to my building now. Just one more stop in Shoreditch, and then it's time to go. Shoreditch is mad; it's a shithole with loads of really posh bits. The posh bits are in fact now most of it, and the shithole is reducing by the day. A few years back I played football around here. We would all get together after work and head down to the pitches under the arches where we would kick lumps out of each other. The side I captained became quite good. We won the league and then the cup the following year. We played in red. I made that decision—the decision being based on the fact that you'll always beat a team in yellow or green if you wear red; it's psychological. I would always fight quite a lot too, during the matches. I had pent up aggression, and it needed to come out; so that's where it came out. I remember back to when I first played a match. The guys at work saw me as a nice, funny, approachable guy; and then when I knocked out one of the opposition, they all looked a little shocked. I say knocked out, he got back up and he was okay. We all shook hands after; I'm sure there were no hard feelings. Okay, it's time for me to go to the office. It's time for me to go.

It's very quiet up here. The weather is bright and clear; the breeze is light, but it's cold. I cried on my way up the fire escape to get here. I cried right until the fire escape door opened and I stepped outside. It was then that the tears just stopped. The traffic is quiet from this distance. All the usual noise is far away from me. It's very quiet in fact. I feel numb and at ease. The cranes are all that I now can see as I step closer whilst I only look up. Tomorrow is my birthday. I'll no longer be thirty-three. I take one more step. Tomorrow is my birthday...my phone starts to buzz in my pocket again. I know who it is, probably found the letters. It's very quiet up here... Tomorrow is my birthday. This is it.

LETTER

Dear Darling,

What I have done is unforgivable. I am not asking for forgiveness as I know it cannot be given. Nor do I deserve it.

Being me has had an effect on you and the children. They and you should not have to have had such poison in your lives. To be a good father and to be a good husband is something that I have failed at repeatedly. If I could explain to you all the feelings that I had, good and bad, then I would have. However, I seem unable to care, not least for myself. "Emotional cripple," as you once rightly said. The jokes are a disguise. The laughing and fun version of me was always replaced by a crying (and at most times drunk) scared little boy. Although throughout all of this, I was unable to come to you, or anyone, for that matter. Everything here is my fault, and I can't ever make anything better.

I know that you'll be a great mother and will meet a more deserving person than that of I. You are also more deserving of course!

On a practical note, I've ensured that the accounts are transferred over and the insurance will go straight to you. The spare keys to my car are in the kitchen drawer, and my car is at the station. I've left it on Talbort Road, so there's no parking fines. My brother will be able to help with anything. He'll understand.

There're additional letters for the boys. They can have them whenever you feel fit to let them, if at all. I'll leave that up to you. Maybe they won't remember me in time and that will be that.

When we met, I fell so much in love. I will always be in love with you. It's not that I ever fell out of love. I don't know what happened. I thought I had everything under control, but I had nothing. Although I had everything.

There's nothing in this for you. There's nothing that I can do to make your life better, nor the kids. It's best that I go. I can't stop the ranting, I can't stop the tears, I can't stop the manic anger that flashes from nowhere nor the dark clouds that all consume. You should not have to be around it, and you'll not need to be anymore.

With all my heart and my messed-up head, I want you to know that I love you and I want you to be loved.

Xx
Bertie

ABOUT THE AUTHOR

Little is known about G. Vanstone; he was once dubbed: *"The Banksy of the book world"*

Glük was born and raised on a south east London council estate. Both parents worked throughout his childhood in the construction and care industries. Growing up on a council estate, it is believed that Glük chose his friends wisely in an aim to not get sucked into the crime that was around him. When Glük was asked to leave school (politely) at the age of 16 he had no qualifications to fall back on. It is thought that he was very capable, but didn't like the authoritarian regime school handed him and was also rather lazy and disruptive.

Before dropping off the radar we know that he attended a local state-run college where he obtained qualifications in Business and Finance and later went on to obtain a degree via remote learning.

The book is believed to be an accurate representation of his life and actions.

Lightning Source UK Ltd.
Milton Keynes UK
UKHW010712310821
389774UK00001B/74

9 781649 521132